The Mystery of God's GOLDEN VESSELS

"If you cannot fly, run. If you cannot run, walk, if you cannot walk. Then crawl. By all means, keep moving."
MARTIN LUTHER KING, JR.

The Mystery of God's GOLDEN VESSELS

Unveiling the mysteries of God's Golden Vessels which will stir up your life, to move you from the valley of stagnancy to the mountain top of mighty men and women of God as you walk in Signs, Wonders and Miracles.

Yves P. Beauvais

The Mystery of God's Golden Vessels
by Yves P. Beauvais

Cover Design by Atinad Designs.

© Copyright 2014

SAINT PAUL PRESS, DALLAS, TEXAS, First Printing, 2014

All rights reserved. No part of this publication may be reproduced, stored in a retrieval system, or transmitted in any form or by any means, electronic, mechanical, photocopying, recording, or otherwise, without the prior permission of the copyright owner, except for brief quotations included in a review of the book.

Unless otherwise identified, Scripture quotations are from New King James Version of the Bible

Holy Bible, New International Version, NIV. Copyright 1973, 1978, 1984, 2011 by Biblica, Inc. used by permission. All rights reserved worldwide.

New Living Translation

Holy Bible, New Living Translation copyright 1996, 2004, 2007 by Tyndale house Foundation. Used by permission of Tyndale House Publishers, Inc.; Carol Stream, Illinois, 60188. All rights reserved.

Take note that the name, satan, and its related names are not capitalized. I prefer not to acknowledge him, even to the point of violating grammatical rules. God hates satan and so do I and everyone of God's Golden Vessels.

ISBN-13: 978-1505658613
ISBN-10: 1505658616

Printed in the U.S.A.

Dedication

This book is dedicated to God the Father, God the Son (Jesus Christ), and to the Holy Spirit; to pastor, Abraham S. Madet, to my lovely, gifted wife, Joy Rose Beauvais, who supported me tirelessly; to prophet Volney Mondelus, Thevenise Auguste, Marvin Antoine, Marcelle Dumervil, Pastor Carline Bien-Aime, to the whole Eleventh Hour Ministry Family all around the world and to my three children: Jemimah, Yochanan Akim, and Prince Joash Beauvais.

I also dedicate this book to those fervently devoted believers whom God is raising up today in the Eleventh Hour Ministry and around the world to destroy the kingdom of darkness and to build the kingdom of God. And to the believers who did not settle for less, but went ahead of us and were used as pure gold in the hands of God. Now we can all imitate Christ and be all that God wants us to be—Golden Vessels.

Contents

Acknowledgements 9
Introduction 11

1. The Art of Willingness 13
2. Gold and Fire 17
3. The Code of Total Agreement 23
4. Brokeness 29
5. Touch Not the Lord's Anointed 33
6. Forgiveness 43
7. Pursue Love 49
8. Seek God's Presence Instead of His Pocket 53
9. His Name 59
10. The Secret Room of Praise, Prayer,
    Dance, & Worship 67
11. A Trustworthy Companion 85
12. Faithful Servants Become Great Leaders 91
13. Fear Not, Your Enemies Have Been Defeated 97
14. Walk in the Power of His Might 103
15. Barricades in Life 117
16. The Purpose of the Enemy Revealed 123
17. The Tenacity of Jesus Christ on Earth 127
18. God Kind of Faith 133
19. The Gifts and the Authority 141
20. It's Time to Arise & Shine 157
21. Shema and Yirah God 161
22. In Closing… 167

If You're Not BORN AGAIN, You're Not Safe! 173
Enter the Prayer Room 175
About the Author 187

Acknowledgements

I would love to thank my lovely wife, Rose Beauvais; my mother, Saintadie Alcide; and my father, Merandieu Beauvais; whom I will continue to honor, respect, and adore forever! A holy kiss to the entire staff of Eleventh Hour Ministry, Four Winds God Kingdom Fellowship. I truly enjoy serving you.

Introduction

♦

> "But in a great house there are not only vessels of gold and of silver, but also of wood and of clay; and some to honour, and some to dishonour. If a man therefore purge himself from these, he shall be a vessel unto honour, sanctified, and meet for the master's use, and prepared unto every good work" (2 Timothy 2:20-21).

Are you determined to aim for a deeper and a greater experience with God? Are you willing to learn from those ordinary men and women who became vessels of honor in the hands of God? If so, you are reading the right book.

There are many Christian books on various subjects, today, but I have not seen any book on the mystery of God's Golden Vessels. It is written out of deep desire that all of God's beloved people would grow to understand the importance of being a Golden Vessel in the hands of God. That's the position He has called all of His children to be in.

This book contains revelations which will stir up your spirit and move you from the valley of zero to the mountain top as mighty men and women of God. There is something unique and explosive about God's Golden Vessels practicing obedience and being willing to dwell in the service of God to help carry out His honorable tasks. This book will challenge you to join the company of sons and daughters of God who are connected to the source of unlimited signs, wonders, and miracles, through their uncommon obedience. It is powerfully presented and illustrated in an easy way. *The Mystery of God's Golden Vessels* is a guide to countless positions of honor right in the hand of the Almighty God. Hallelujah!

CHAPTER 1

The Art of Willingness

◆

WHAT TYPE OF VESSEL ARE YOU WILLING TO BE?

Golden vessel is willing to do whatever it takes to honor God. Martin Luther King, Jr once said, "If you cannot fly, run. If you cannot run, walk, if you cannot walk. Then crawl. By all means, keep moving". The choice is yours. God created you as a free agent. You can choose when to eat and when not to eat. When to go to bed or when to watch TV. You can choose the type of vessel you want to be. For God does not show any favoritism Romans 2:11. And He is no a respecter of persons.

If you are a born again believer, and washed in the blood of the lamb, then you are God's extension here on earth. There is no favoritism in Him. He is not focus on your past sins, failures, past rejection and experiences to use you, but he desires a yielding vessel, one who is thirsty for more of an intimate friendship. Friend, I am here to tell you that you are not any different from any of the mighty men and women you read about in the Holy Bible. These men only yielded themselves into the bosom of God through the channel of the Holy Spirit, who enabled them to be used as God's Golden Vessels for His honorable services.

All treasures of life is hidden in Christ Jesus. "That our hearts might be comforted, being knit together in love, and unto all riches of the full assurance of understanding, to the acknowledgement of the mystery of God, and of the Father, and of Christ; in whom are hid all the treasures of wisdom and knowledge" Colossians 2:2-3. Everything you could possibly desire, including God's golden vessel, will come through obedience and relationship with Jesus Christ.

When we give our lives to Christ, we are translated out of the kingdom of darkness and into the kingdom of Light and so we become a type of vessel for service. Some are **clay, wooden, silver** and **gold vessels**. From amongst them, God is seeking the one who makes himself available for honorable work which He called Golden Vessels.

Now, let us look at the nature of the clay and wooden vessels. These types of vessels are like people who are in the house of God, but who have no desire to grow into the deep things of God. They go to church late and complain, gossip, and murmur about everything. Nothing is working properly for them, yet they will not give any input on how to fix the situation. They are double-minded, hypocritical, easy to be broken, and very fragile in the flesh. Clay and wooden vessels fight over every little thing. These types will and may even kill their fellow brothers for their religious rituals or activities. They're not focusing on God to build up the kingdom of God. Clay and wooden vessels bring confusion in the body of Christ, and sometimes you cannot tell whether or not they are believers. They talk from what they know not. They allow the devil to use them easily. Clay and wooden vessels are like the carnal-minded. They bring more problems into the body of Christ.

Clay and wooden vessels are like people who are not passionate enough to drink the pure milk, which is the Word of God, to get them where God wants them to be. They are babies in their faith and they are easily tossed by any wind of doctrine. They're constantly arguing about earthly things. The problem with them is that they refuse to let God transform their way of thinking; therefore, they cannot eat solid food. Today God is telling us to move up from clay, wooden, silver into golden vessels. Every human being must decide for himself which kind of vessel he wants to be in the hands of the Almighty God.

God is looking for gold and silver vessels to use in an honorable position. He is looking for a group of people who will impact their environment in ways that glorify Him. Golden vessels carry the glory and the righteousness of God wherever they go with great signs and wonders for the Lord. They are stable in God. They are exercising their authority in God. They know who they are in God. They carry the nature of their Father God. They are problem solver. Demons and evil works cannot stop them from fulfilling God's agenda.

And so in a great house there are not only <u>*vessels of gold*</u> and of silver, but also of wood and of clay, and some to honour, and some to dishonor (2 Timothy 2:20).

To be a <u>vessel of honour</u>, sanctified and profitable to the Master, one must yield himself to the Holy Spirit and be eager to comprehend thoroughly the following:

- Gold and Fire
- The Code of Total Agreement
- Brokenness
- Seeking God Presence, not His Wallet
- Walking in the Power of His Might
- Shema and Yirah God
- and much more

As you go through the depths of this book, my prayer is that you will open your spirit to comprehend and grasp the revelation God has given me through His Holy Spirit and accept the tangible touch of the splendor of being in His hand as a vessel of honor. Let's go for the golden level!

CHAPTER 2

Gold and Fire

♦

Why did God use Golden Vessels for His honorable services? Gold is a good conductor of heat and electricity and a strong reflector of infrared radiation. Gold can be easily beaten and heated to bring about its purification without damage. If you try a wood vessel in a fire, it will burn to ashes. Fire causes clay vessels to deform and melt. But the nature of a gold vessel is such that it stands up to the fierce heat of fire. Fire purifies the gold and makes it last for years. Gold is not affected by fire, nor by acid.

Fire is the nature of God. The Bible declares that God is a consuming fire. In other words, God's nature is similar to that of gold, and so anyone who wishes to be at that level of honor for God's services must step into the golden level. Our works, and our good deeds, will be tested by fire. Elisha experienced the fire and he used it to stop witchcraft activities in his time. You, too, can use that fire within in the Name of Jesus to destroy the works of darkness in your life. In 2 Kings 1:10, Elijah answered the captain, "If I am a man of God, may fire come down from heaven and consume you and your fifty men!" Then fire fell from heaven and consumed the captain and his men.

A lukewarm or a powerless Christian life style is not of God. Why? God is a consuming fire and He made His servants flames of fire; therefore, as born again Christians, we ought to be too hot for the devil to gaze upon. Our talk should be talk of fire; our walk should be walk of fire. Everything about us must be tested by fire. The Israelites could not face the fire because of their complaining and murmuring attitude, and so when God called them to come up so that He could speak to them, they were afraid of the fire. Fire is not an acquaintance with sin. It will destroy sin.

Fire is there in our lives to either purify or to burn. It will purify us to be the gold vessel we need to be in God's hands. Fire will burn sin out of our lives. Fire destroys the flesh.

The devil is afraid of fire. That's the reason you and I need to always be on fire and be saturated with the Holy Ghost. Sometimes when I am casting demon spirits out of an individual, the evil spirits would cry out, "Burning!" "Burning"! the person would literally act like someone who is burning with fire. Why? Evil spirits see the fire and they know what the fire is going to do if they stand there one extra minute. They understood the dangerous of fire in the life of the children of God. Fire cast them out of their victims. Friend, we need fire of the Holy Ghost everywhere we go. You may not be able to see it with your eyes, but when your life is on fire, demon spirits know it and they are ready to flee from your presence. Glory to God.

John the Baptist said: "I baptize you with water. But one more powerful than I will come, the thongs of whose sandals I am not worthy to untie. He will baptize you with the Holy Spirit and with fire."

Without that fire in your life, demon spirits will mock you and it will be impossible to be effective in your walk with God. To dismantle evil spirits, you need that fire. If not, they will sit on your head and mock you like they did to the seven sons of Sceva:

Acts 19: *Seven sons of Sceva tried to invoke the name of the Lord Jesus over those who were demon-possessed. They would say, "In the name of the Jesus whom Paul preaches, I command you to come out." One day the evil spirit answered them, "Jesus I know, and Paul I know about, but who are you?" Then the man who had the evil spirit jumped on them and overpowered them all. He gave them such a beating that they ran out of the house naked and bleeding.*

These seven sons of Sceva were cold like a frozen turkey. We need the Holy Ghost and fire to quench the works of darkness. The evil spirits know if you are serious in God or if you're playing church. The evil spirits answered, "Jesus I know, and Paul I know about, but who are you?

Are you ready for that fire?

Jesus Christ is ready and willing to baptize all of God's children in the Holy Ghost and fire. That fire destroy the works of darkness in our lives, and it enables us to destroy the deeds of witchcraft upon the life of other people around us as well. God uses fire to test the work of men. The fire will burn your bad attitudes and your selfish behaviors. It will burn to ashes all unclean spirits tormenting your life. Do you need the fire? Say Lord I need the fire.

This fire is real. It guards your life from the tricks or schemes of the enemy. It will kill sicknesses and diseases in your body. This fire will burn unclean spirits in your life to ashes. We need the fire. That fire allows you to be dead to self and to be alive for Jesus Christ. It purifies and changes you from one step of glory to another step of glory. That fire gives a different presence to your being and a closer contact in your walk with God. That's why God is seeking for Golden Vessels to use for His honorable service. Golden Vessels are not afraid of the fire. They love it.

The fire of God in your life will be seen in your

relationship with God and with other people as well. That fire gives you boldness to spread the Word and your prayer relationship will change because of its presence in your life. You will have the chance to operate in spiritual gifts to help others. What we need is more of His presence of fire. The more you walk in the presence of God, the more that fire will purify you into the very image of His Son, Jesus Christ.

In the days of the apostles, the church willingly went through the fire, while the church of today is complacent and likes the comfort zone, which hinders it from impacting this generation. It is extremely important for us to climb the ladder to get to that golden level, because only those who can withstand the fire will occupy a position of honor to serve the Master, Almighty God.

CHAPTER 3

The Code of Total Agreement

◆

How can two walk together, except they be agreed? (Amos 3:3).

It is dangerous not to be in agreement with God. Agreement with God is a secret to be a golden vessel level. The Bible declares one can chase a thousand, And two put ten thousand to flight. One man of you puts to flight a thousand, since it is the Lord your God who fights for you, just as he promised you. Pay close attention to the word. If one can put to flight a thousand, what about two, three or ten people, then nothing can withhold it. Matthews 18:19 makes a bold statement about agreement when it says: "Again I say to you, if two of you agree on earth about anything they ask, it will be done for them by my Father in heaven".

Agreement with God means you are in one accord

with Him; one mind; harmony in belief; beloved it is in our best interest to be in total agreement with God instead of being disagree with Him. Some people are mad with God because of their lack of knowledge, God is always looking for our best interest. He wants to save. He wants to heal. He wants to deliver and so forth. During my years in ministry, I encounter people who want to be used by God, yet disagree with Him in almost everything; they are not willing to accept the principles set forth by God for them to abide. To be in total agreement with God requires that we:

(1) **Accept God in our lives for Who He is.** We must accept, Honor and value Him, be willing to abide by His principles and His Word, and be quick to do His will. His will is His Word, Jesus Christ. God is not a man, so he does not lie. He is not human, so he does not change his mind. Has he ever spoken and failed to act? Has he ever promised and not carried it through?

When we do what the word says - that's agreement with God.

(2) **Be willing to gaze upon His Son, Jesus Christ.** "Fixing our eyes on Jesus, the author and the finisher of our faith, who for the joy set before Him endured the cross, despising the shame, and is set down at the right hand of the throne of God" (Hebrews 12:2). Take off your eyes from the thing of this world; from the craving of this world. But look unto Jesus, the writer of your life, and let Him make any necessary corrections and

changes according to the Book as you sit and rest in Him, then you will see all your enemies become your footstools. It is that simple.

(3) **Labor with God to win souls.**

1 Corinthians 3:9: "For we are labourers together with God: ye are God's husbandry, ye are God's building."

We are working with God, the Great I AM! Some people are working for God and not with God. There is a big difference, God wants people to work with Him, meaning we are doing it together, He is the boss, not us. We listen to His advice because He knows all things, not us. Saints, we can be true soul winners and bring billions into the kingdom of God when we labour with Him. In Proverbs 11:30, the Bible declares, *"He who wins souls is wise."* Be wise! Win souls for we are laboring with God. We cannot fail when we are laboring with God. He will never leave us nor forsake us! He invested in us His precious Holy Spirit who will lead us throughout the entire course of life. He empowered us with strength from above—an ability to drive the vehicle of life stress free. By God's grace and mighty power, we have been given the privilege of serving Him by spreading this Good News.

In Luke 4:43 Jesus said: "I must preach the good news of the kingdom of God to the other towns as well; for I was sent for this purpose." And he came and preached peace to you who were far away, and peace to those who were near" Jesus was laboring with God.

Apostle Paul labourer with God. He made this declaration in Ephesians 3:8-13:

> **Though I am the least deserving of all God's people, he graciously gave me the privilege of telling the Gentiles about the endless treasures available to them in Christ.**
>
> **I was chosen to explain to everyone this *mysterious* plan that God, the Creator of all things, had kept secret from the beginning. God's purpose in all this was to use the church to display his wisdom in its rich variety to all the unseen rulers and authorities in the heavenly places.**
>
> **This was his eternal plan, which he carried out through Christ Jesus our Lord. Because of Jesus Christ and our faith in him, we can now come boldly and confidently into God's presence. So please don't lose heart because of my trials here. I am suffering for you, so you should feel honored.**

(4) **Pray for spiritual growth.** Agreement with God demands spiritual growth. We cannot remain babes for the rest of our Christian life. We must grow spiritually. Apostle Paul said in Ephesians 3:14-20: When I think of all this, I fall to my knees and pray to the Father, the

Creator of everything in heaven and on earth. I pray that from his glorious, unlimited resources he will empower you with inner strength through his Spirit. Then Christ will make his home in your hearts as you trust in him. Your roots will grow down into God's love and keep you strong.

And may you have the power to understand, as all God's vessels should, how wide, how long, how high, and how deep his love is. May you experience the love of Christ, though it is too great to understand fully. And you are complete in him, which is the head of all principality and power. Apostle Paul asked that the Spirit of God would strengthen the church with might to do the work of the Kingdom and to carry on the great commission of the Gospel of our Lord and Savior Jesus Christ.

(5) **Be quick to repent from every wicked way.** Total agreement with God demands true and quick repentance in the heart. It means complete turning from our own direction to God's direction. It is leaving our deceitful way for God's way. It is seeking the way of God to fulfill His desire upon your life. One of the best examples of true repentance is found in Luke 15:11-32 when the prodigal son said "in his heart, 'I will arise and go to my father,' then he got up and went back." He turned around to return home. He forsook his old way of living to abide by his father's principles.

"And he arose and came to his father. But when

he was still a great way off, his father saw him and had compassion, and ran and fell on his neck and kissed him. And the son said to him, 'Father, I have sinned against heaven and in your sight, and am no longer worthy to be called your son'" (Luke 15:20-21).

Repentance is incomplete until you begin to travel in the new direction set forth by God, the Creator of the Universe. Repentance is a firm decision followed by godly action. Be in total agreement with God no matter the cost. That's the life of God's Golden Vessels.

CHAPTER 4

Brokeness

♦

Trust in the LORD with all thine heart; and lean not unto thine own understanding. In all thy ways acknowledge him, and he shall direct thy paths. Be not wise in thine own eyes: fear the LORD, and depart from evil. (Proverbs 3:5-7)

Brokenness is essential for us to become the vessels that we ought to be. The Holy Spirit's job is to transform us into people who please God, but we must yield ourselves to Him. A brokenness attitude positions one to be a candidate for honorable services. It is not what you can do with yourself, rather, it is what Jesus Christ is able to do with you when you surrender yourself totally unto Him. God would take that which appears to you as nothing, that which is dirty and filthy, and He will bless it, break it, and multiply it to be a blessing to millions. The question is: Are you willing to be broken in the hands of God?

In Mark 6:41 we read: *"And when He had taken the five loaves and the two fish, He looked up to heaven, blessed and broke the loaves, and gave them to His disciples to set before them; and the two fish He divided among them all."*

The Holy Spirit seeks those who are willing to be broken, so that He can use them for mighty and unusual works. He will multiply you and make you a blessing to nations. For example, He took Saul of Tarsus who was a murderer, a gossiper, a criminal, and He purged all the filthiness out of him, even changing his name to Paul, and used him as His Golden Vessel for great and mighty works in ministry. The New Testament, most of which was written by Paul, testifies to this.

Brokenness means leaving old habits, old attitudes, and an old lifestyle. Sometimes it may mean leaving your unfriendly friends and family members. It may mean walking away from secret sins. It can be very painful when you have to leave things that you were used to; but for one who would be God's Golden Vessel, it is a must.

Brokenness means your total obedience to following Christ Examples. You have to walk in obedience of His calling upon your life in order to see great results. You have to obey His vision and His perfect plan for your life. Paul stated: "I am crucified with Christ: nevertheless I live; yet not I, but Christ liveth in me: and the life which I now live in the flesh I live by the faith of the Son of God, who loved me, and gave himself for me." Why? Because when you are in a state of brokenness, you live for Him and Him alone. His desires become your desires. If He tells you to get up, you'll get up without asking Him any questions. If you are desiring to become a Golden Vessel you will go through a brokenness stage in your life.

When my wife and I decided to go deeper into the work of ministry, people said all kinds of evil things against us; even close family and friends ran away from us. They put all kinds of labels on us to stop us in our walk with God and when I questioned the Holy Spirit about it, He told me they did much more to Jesus Christ, the Savior of humanity. He told me, if you remain faithful unto God and walk in the fear of the Lord, all your enemies will confess that God is truly with you.

"Blessed are you when people forsake you for my Name's sake." Jesus told us through His Word that He was a victim of lies, envy, and deceit. He suffered hate, and through the years withstood being forgotten. As the Lamb, He was slain. Isaiah 53:3 declares: "He is despised and rejected by men, a Man of sorrows and acquainted with grief and we hid, as it were, our faces from Him; He was despised, and we did not esteem Him."

Jesus was led by the Spirit into the wilderness to be tempted there by the devil. For forty days and forty nights he fasted and became very hungry (Matthew 4:1-2 NLT).

In your brokenness page of life, the Holy Spirit will always ask you to do things that the carnal and natural mind are not willing to do. The Holy Spirit may ask you to go into the wilderness to spend time alone with Him. He will ask you to give up your reputation, pride, hatred, envy, and gossip to deal with the "me, myself, and I" mentality so that He can move you a step higher, but the flesh will try its best to resist it. As a Golden Vessel you will have to be obedient to the Holy Spirit and walk according to his will. The devil may use people who are not willing to be broken by the hand of God to rise up against you. But, just press on! Keep on looking to Jesus, the author and finisher of your faith. He will never leave nor forsake you, for your obedience to His voice will always lead you to a place of greatness.

The brokenness stages allow you to prepare yourself to walk with dominion over sin, over the flesh and its selfish desires. That is why the Golden Vessel is qualified to do the Master's honorable work, for it is his will to please God and nothing of this world will stop him. Golden vessel delights and surrenders himself totally in the fear of the Lord and God lifts him up in due time. And they respect the Lord's anointed.

Write down three areas of your spiritual life that you want to see a change:

1. _____
2. _____
3. _____

CHAPTER 5

Touch Not the Lord's Anointed

◆

"Do not touch my anointed ones; do my prophets no harm" (Psalm 105:15).

Golden vessels honor the Lord's anointed because they are also anointed. Touch can be both physical and spiritual. The moment people begin to talk negatively about God's anointed, they put themselves in an unfavorable position with God. God will not remain silent about it. When you slander God's anointed, you disturb the affairs of God. You are fighting not with that individual directly, but with God Himself.

God's Golden Vessels are the apple of His eyes. Do not disturb them! Do not take a second to talk bad about them for it will be to your disadvantage.

They took Peter and put him in prison and threatened him not to speak the name of Jesus. They wanted to kill him because of the Word. They plotted to make an end of his life and his ministry. But Gamaliel, one of the council members, stood up and told the Pharisees not to touch the Lord's anointed unless they wanted to fight with God [emphasized added. When you touch the Lord's anointed with evil, whether you do it physically, verbally, or non-verbally, you are only fighting with God. And anyone who fights with God is wasting their time, for God cannot lose.

Jesus puts it this way, in Acts 4:11: "He is the STONE WHICH WAS REJECTED by you, THE BUILDERS, but WHICH BECAME THE CHIEF CORNER stone." Whoever falls on this stone will be broken to pieces; but on whoever it falls, it will grind him to powder (Matthew 21:44). We are the living stone of God through Christ (1 Peter 2:5). Touch not the Lord's golden vessels.

Miriam and Aaron spoke against Moses. They criticized him because of the lady he married and as a result Miriam became leprous. God was listening to their evil talk; Miriam suffered great consequences.

Miriam and Aaron spoke against Moses because of the Ethiopian woman whom he had married; for he had married an Ethiopian woman. So they said, "Has the LORD indeed spoken only through Moses? Has He not spoken through us also?"

And the LORD heard it (Numbers 12:1-2 NKJV).

When someone is anointed, God has smeared or consecrated him. In other words, God placed a mark upon that person's life with the purpose to minister to His people. When people begin to mess with God's anointed, they are messing with God Himself. In other words, they are playing with CONSUMING FIRE.

Forty-two kids were seriously injured and died because they were mocking Elisha, the anointed of the Lord.

> **From there Elisha went up to Bethel. As he was walking along the road, some boys came out of the town and jeered at him. "Get out of here, baldy!" they said. "Get out of here, baldy!" He turned around, looked at them and called down a curse on them in the name of the LORD. Then two bears came out of the woods and mauled forty-two of the boys (2 Kings 2:23-24).**

When God anoints someone, He puts His Spirit upon the life of that person for a specific purpose or assignment. We owe that person respect and honor, because when we honor him, we honor God. When we dishonor God's anointed, we dishonor God.

If that person is not doing his job or if he is in disobedience to God, touch him not, for the same God who placed him in office can remove him. So avoid trying to be god over the life of the Lord's anointed.

Proverbs 24:16 states: "For though the righteous fall seven times, they rise again." It is not your responsibility nor mine to talk negatively or gossip about any man or woman of God because the Lord is listening to every word we speak against His anointed. David understood that principle. He said in 1 Samuel 26:9, "who can stretch out his hand against the Lord's anointed, and be guiltless?"

The Prophet Nathan also understood that principle: When David sinned, Prophet Nathan came, not to boss David around or to disrespect him, but he humbly spoke the Word of God to David. He used wisdom to speak to him.

2 Samuel 12:1-15 says:

Then the Lord sent Nathan to David. And he came to him, and said to him: "There were two men in one city, one rich and the other poor. The rich man had exceedingly many flocks and herds. But the poor man had nothing, except one little ewe lamb which he had bought and nourished; and it grew up together with him and with his children. It ate of his own food and drank from his own cup and lay in his bosom; and it was like a daughter to him.

And a traveler came to the rich man, who refused to take from his own flock and from his own herd to prepare one for the wayfaring man who had come to him; but he took the poor man's lamb

and prepared it for the man who had come to him."

So David's anger was greatly aroused against the man, and he said to Nathan, "As the Lord lives, the man who has done this shall surely die! And he shall restore fourfold for the lamb, because he did this thing and because he had no pity."

Then Nathan said to David, "You are the man! Thus says the Lord God of Israel: 'I anointed you king over Israel, and I delivered you from the hand of Saul. I gave you your master's house and your master's wives into your keeping, and gave you the house of Israel and Judah. And if that had been too little, I also would have given you much more!

"'Why have you despised the commandment of the Lord, to do evil in His sight? You have killed Uriah the Hittite with the sword; you have taken his wife to be your wife, and have killed him with the sword of the people of Ammon. Now therefore, the sword shall never depart from your house, because you have despised Me, and have taken the wife of Uriah the Hittite to be your wife.'

Thus says the Lord: 'Behold, I will raise up adversity against you from your own house; and I will take your wives before your eyes and give them to your neighbor, and he shall lie with your

wives in the sight of this sun. For you did it secretly, but I will do this thing before all Israel, before the sun.'"

So David said to Nathan, "I have sinned against the Lord." And Nathan said to David, "The Lord also has put away your sin; you shall not die. However, because by this deed you have given great occasion to the enemies of the Lord to blaspheme, the child also who is born to you shall surely die."

Then Nathan departed to his house.

Did you see it?

Anyone trying to engage you in talking against any man or woman of God, ask him to pray for that man or woman of God. If refuse, you need to walk away from that conversation so that you will not be a partaker of their sins. Do not share in the sins of others. Keep yourself pure (1 Timothy 5:22).

No matter how wicked someone may be, you still owe him love and not evil. For we overcome evil with good. God knows how to avenge for His children; so let Him do it.

1 Peter 2:13-19 says: "For the Lord's sake, respect all human authority—whether the king as head of state, or the officials he has appointed; For the king has sent them to punish those who do wrong and to honor those

who do right. Do what they tell you—not only if they are kind and reasonable, but even if they are cruel. For God is pleased with you when you do what you know is right and patiently endure unfair treatment."

WE ARE CHRIST'S AMBASSADORS

We are Christ's ambassador (2 Corinthians 5:20), meaning H put us in a position of honor. We can speak on His behalf. We can speak and understand His language. We represent a higher power, a kingdom full of authority, the kingdom of the Lord of lords and the King of kings. God has granted us a level of authority. We have the ability to cut off the source of living of those who wrongly touch us.

"He called down famine on the land and destroyed all their supplies of food" (Psalm 105:16).

Examine yourself to see if you have talked bad and evil about any of the Lord's anointed, be quickly if so repent!!

Michal, David's wife, was cursed. She became barren because she despised David in her heart and so she remained childless throughout her entire life. Second Samuel 6:14 says: "David danced before the LORD with all his might; and David was wearing a linen ephod." In verse 16 we read: "Michal, Saul's daughter, looked through a window and saw King David leaping and whirling before the LORD; and she despised him in her heart."

In Acts 13:6-12 we saw Apostle Paul cursed Elymas with a blindness because he withstood him, and sought to turn the proconsul, Sergius Paulus, away from the faith or from hearing the Word of God.

It does not matter if he is a bishop, big-shot, pastor, apostle, prophet, evangelist, etc. As long someone has been anointed by God, then we owe him respect. We are not allowed to touch him, nor to do him any harm because God, as the chief Master, is watching over His ambassador.

HONORING YOUR LEADERS

I have discovered even among believers we sometimes fail to discern whether or not a man or a woman is of God. However, that woman discerned that Elisha was a holy man of God. She said to her husband, "Let's build a small room for him on the roof and furnish it with a bed, a table, a chair, and a lamp. Then he will have a place to stay whenever he comes by." Even though she was a wealthy woman, her money could not buy her a child of her own. She needed favor from God and from the man of God.

The man of God prophesied upon her and released a child to be born of her. He destroyed the spirit of barrenness that kept that woman in bondage for years.

Do you see it? Second Kings 4:15 says, "Elisha said to her as she stood in the doorway, 'Next year at this time you will be holding a son in your arms!'"

God has entrusted His Golden Vessels with great power and authority to release things that may have been withheld for years. When you come in contact with such a man of God, your life can be shifted in a totally new direction. In other words, when you honor a man of God, you simply agree with him or her for your miracle. Do not be deceived when I say man of God, I am not talking about people who just carry a big Bible and go places taking advantage of others. Or people who are destroying the body of Christ for personal interest. But I am talking about men and women of integrity who minister with compassion, love, and who seek after God's heart. You will know them by their fruits (Galatians 5:22).

God told us to test every spirit to know whether or not it is from Him. But He did NOT tell us to be suspicious. He said Test, to test you must know the word and be able to listen and hear the voice of the Holy Spirit.

First John Chapter Four tells us how to test spirits: "Beloved, do not believe every spirit, but test the spirits to see whether they are from God, because many false prophets have gone out into the world. By this you know the Spirit of God: every spirit that confesses that Jesus Christ has come in the flesh is from God and every spirit that does not confess Jesus is not from God; this is the spirit of the antichrist, of which you have heard that it is coming, and now it is already in the world.... "

You will know the God's golden vessels when their work are LOVE-DRIVEN. Jesus put it this way, you will know the tree by its fruit. Jesus was the ultimate example of God's Golden Vessel on earth. He moved by love. Every move He made was driven by love and compassion. Jesus said, "By their fruit you will recognize them. Every good tree bears good fruit, but a bad tree bears bad fruit. A good tree cannot bear bad fruit, and a bad tree cannot bear good fruit. Every tree that does not bear good fruit is cut down and thrown into the fire" (Matthew 7:16-19).

It is love that moves God's Golden Vessels to heal the sick, cast out devils, raise the dead, feed the hungry, etc. If we are struggling to do what God is asking us to do it is because we are not walking in love. When our live are driven by His love, nothing in His Word will be too difficult for us to do.

Golden Vessels do not argue with God, they simply submit and obey to His Word.

CHAPTER 6

Forgiveness

◆

Be kind and compassionate to one another, forgiving each other, just as in Christ God forgave you (Ephesians 4:32).

Golden vessels have a heart to forgive. They are very quick to forgive others. Many people even scholars talk about forgiveness, they teach, preach, and sing about it, yet not all of us experience or live it out in our lives. Forgiveness is not "forget-ness". It is not pretending. It is not acting in hypocrisy. It is not acting as though everything is well. Forgiveness is what Jesus did on Calvary as seen in His words: "Father, forgive them for they know not what they're doing." It means you free and release the person from the prison of your heart. Moses did it. He forgave Pharaoh and His brother and sister Miriam after they have sinned against him. Stephen did it when he was stoned.

When true forgiveness is taking place you will not

hold any grudges against the person who wronged you. It is like someone who cuts you with a knife: you will remember what happened whenever you see the mark or scars, but you will not have any bitterness toward the person who did it to you; instead, you will show love and seek peace. You can boldly say, "seventy seven times I forgive you, sister or brother, and I love you."

Forgiveness is a choice. We choose of our own free will to forgive or not to forgive. It is our choice, but it worth doing it. Yes, sometimes it may be very hard and difficult to forgive those who have hurt, harmed, wronged, or betrayed us. But, if we make a firm decision of our own free will to forgive, God is right there in His infinite love, grace, and mercy, to help us to forgive.

Yes, we can forgive. The Bible commands us to forgive one another not just seven times, but seventy times seven. That's 490 times. Matthew 18:21-22 says: *"Lord, how many times shall I forgive my brother or sister who sins against me? Up to seven times?" Jesus answered, "I tell you, not seven times, but seventy times seven."*

Forgiveness is clear. When you freely release the victim from your heart you will experience peace and love in your heart. Your heart will fill with love and you will see the victim the same way that God sees him without hypocrisy. That's forgiveness.

You may say, Pastor Yves, I cannot forgive him! He killed my friends, he betrayed me, he beats me, he destroyed my marriage, he ruin my reputation and the list goes on. Well, to tell you the truth, the flesh will not want to release someone who has done you wrong, free of charge. The flesh wants the victim to pay the price without giving him a chance to repent. The flesh will cry "revenge"; but the Holy Spirit in you is willing and He wants you to forgive. Why? It is in the perfect will of God, our Father, to forgive one another. And remember, in spite of all the wrong you and I did to God, He still loves us and He forgave us of all of our sins.

Mark 11:25 declares: If you hold anything against anyone, *forgive him*, so that your Father in heaven may forgive you your sins. And Romans 3:23 says, "All have sinned and fallen short of the glory of God."

When you forgive, you are opening up your heart to the uttermost fruit of the Spirit of God to operate into your life. You give room for peace, joy, gentleness, kindness, and faithfulness to reside within you. You take away the mud of bitterness, and replace it with the joy of the Lord.

THE PROBLEM WITH AN UNFORGIVING HEART

Unforgiving is an invention of satan. An unforgiving heart welcomes sickness, bitterness, and wrath, which prevents love from operating in your heart as it should.

An unforgiving heart gives satan a legal right to torment you. And you cannot receive much from God when you are not forgiving others because you have a demonic weapon in your hands. Instead of being open to trust and love, you find yourself suspicious of the motivations of others and you keep fleeing instead of advancing in the trust and love of God.

If God can forgive us of all the unrighteous things we have committed against Him, we should also forgive our fellow brothers and sisters no matter what he/she has done wrong. The secret of forgiveness is that when you forgive you close satan out, and welcome God inside. Therefore, if God is in, you will only see victory, triumph, and celebration. But if you keep satan in, you will only experience torment, fear, bitterness, etc.

"Who is a God like you, who pardons sin and forgives the transgression of the remnant of his inheritance? You do not stay angry forever but delight to show mercy. You will again have compassion on us; you will tread our sins underfoot and hurl all our iniquities into the depths of the sea" (Malachi 7:18-19).

You cannot be a vessel of honor in the hands of God if you refuse to forgive your brothers, sisters and/or anyone who sinned against you. In fact, you cannot achieve great things in God if you hold people captive in your heart. Forgive one another for this is right.

Stephen in the book of Acts forgave while he was

being stoned to death. "And they cast him out of the city and stoned him. And the witnesses laid down their clothes at the feet of a young man named Saul. And they stoned Stephen as he was calling on God and saying, 'Lord Jesus, receive my spirit.' Then he knelt down and cried out with a loud voice, '<u>Lord, do not charge them with this sin</u>;' And when he had said this, he fell asleep" (Acts 7:58-60).

God forgave us of our sins in spite of all we have done to Him. "He hath not dealt with us after our sins; nor rewarded us according to our iniquities. For as the heaven is high above the earth, so great is His mercy toward them that fear Him. As far as the east is from the west, so far hath He removed our transgressions from us" (Psalm 103:10-12).

In these verses, we see that no matter what our sins are, in His great loving and tender mercy, God has removed them from us, as far as the east is from the west. If we leave the north pole headed south, we will reach the south pole, and then if we continue on, we will find ourselves headed north. But if we head east we will just keep going around the earth, never reaching west. That is how far God removes our sin from us.

The Lord wants us to forgive and be rooted and grounded in His love and to have a sweetness of spirit like our Savior, Jesus Christ of Nazareth. Forgive one another and go for God's love.

Pray this prayer: *Holy Father, in the Name of Jesus, I* *repent of any unforgiveness that is in my heart toward anybody that has sinned against me. This day, of my own free will, I choose to forgive every body no matter how they may have wronged me. I forgive (name of individual) for every word spoken and every deed committed that hurt or harmed me or my family. I ask, Father God, that you cleanse me with the Blood of Jesus. I also forgive myself, for the unforgiveness I have harbored toward anyone.*

Witchcraft spirits, I speak to you: In the Name of Jesus, I rebuke you, I renounce you and your works in my life. In so doing, I have stripped you of all authority, power, and/or right to torment me. In the Name of Jesus, I take authority over you and cast you out. As you leave my life, today, you will take all the pain, sickness, disease, migraine headaches, stiffness, bitterness, hatred, and hurts you have put on me. In the Name of Jesus, leave now!

Holy Father, I thank You that as of today I am completely free physically, mentally, and emotionally from all hidden works of the enemy in my life in the name of Jesus. Amen and Amen!

CHAPTER 7

Pursue Love

◆

Love is not just in the lip but in sincere action from the heart.

God's Golden Vessel thrives to walk and dwell in love. *Love is the heart of God in action.* Love moves heaven. Love cast out devils. Love changes lives. If you speak all the languages on earth, including the tongues of angels; if you could perform the greatest miracles ever, but not walk in LOVE, then you miss the mark. You are wasting your time. Why? Because love is God. As God's Vessels we must understand this principle and move by love in order to continue carrying the assignment given by our heavenly Father.

First Corinthians 13 declares: "Though I speak with the tongues of men and of angels, but have not love, I have become sounding brass or a clanging cymbal. And though I have the gift of prophecy, and understand all mysteries and all knowledge, and though I have all faith, so that I could remove mountains, but have not love, I am nothing. And though I bestow all my goods to feed the poor, and though I give my body to be burned, but have not love, it profits me nothing."

If all done without the love of God, then it is flesh, and the flesh cannot please God. God is love. He loves us so much that He sent his Son to die for a crooked and a perverted generation. Whoever lives in love lives in God (1 John 4:16 NIV). Because you love Him, you will love your neighbors, even your worst enemies. Because of God's love flowing through you for Him, you will do anything God commands you to do.

Love is not lust. It is not grudging. It is not jealous. It is not quarrelsome. Love is patient. Love is kind. It does not envy. It does not boast in itself. It is not proud. Love lifts up others higher than self. Love is the vehicle to move you into the gift of the Spirit. Love will push you to pray for the sick to be healed, ask God to cast out devils, and prophesy over someone else's life. Amen.

How can I have more of His love in my life? Some may think that we need to pray that God would give us more love. Or they may say that we just don't have the love of God as we ought to. Since the love of God has been shed abroad in our hearts, if a person doesn't seem to have love, he just has to learn to walk in the light of what he already has. That's where the problem is: We are not walking in the light of what we already have. The truth is, we are one with God. God is love and whoever lives in love, lives in God. When you and I gave our hearts to God, God came and dwelt in us, and so we are already have love inside of us. We just need to understand that and walk in the light of the truth. Know the truth and the truth shall make you free.

The Bible says, "We know that we have passed from death to life, because we love the brethren." And if we're saved, we've got the love of God in our hearts because the Bible says the love of God has been shed abroad in our hearts by the Holy Ghost (1 John 3:14; Rom 5:5).

It is not a matter of crying to God for more love, because He's already given every believer the measure of love, just as He's already given every believer the measure of faith. It's just a matter of stirring up and using what's already on the inside!

If you're born again, saved, washed with the blood, you already have a measure of love. You can pray until you are blue in the face that God would give you more love, but the love you have will never be increased until you feed it on God's Word and exercise it so it can develop. Give and it shall be given unto you. Give love and you shall see great release and change in your life. The day you accepted Jesus Christ as your Lord and Savior, you received His love, His joy, and His peace, and if you can just exercise what you already have, then it will be increased. The Holy One who is inside of you is LOVE. Flow with Him. He wants you to seek first His presence, instead of His wallet.

CHAPTER 8

Seek God's Presence Instead of His Pocket

◆

Seek is to look for attentiveness; to search for with undivided attention.

The passion of God's Golden Vessels is to seek His presence, not His pocket. To seek God's presence requires your undivided attention, obedient and trust. Your eyes need to be off the pleasures of the world to focus on Him. You will miss God if your mind is busy on the cares of this world. You ought to seek Him as though you were seeking for water to quench your thirst or seeking for food to relieve your hunger.

God put it this way: "…those who seek me find me." I rewards those who earnestly seek Me. "For everyone who asks receives; the one who SEEKS finds."

David, in Psalm 63:1, declared: "You, God, are my God, (earnestly I seek you; I thirst for you, my whole being longs for you, in a dry and parched land where there is no water."

We must seek His presence with thanksgiving and praise. Singing to God causes us to dwell in the midst of praise. Praise is pleasing to God as it represents the fruit of our relationship with Him. "Let us offer the sacrifice of praise to God continually, that is, the fruit of our lips giving thanks to His Name."

What most people do not understand is that failure to earnestly seek God will stop the flow of the Holy Spirit in our lives. You cannot seek while you are in a hurry; it is time to stop whatever you were doing to earnestly seek God.

God said: "You will seek me and find me when you seek me with all your heart" (Jeremiah 29:13 NIV).

The truth is when you find God, you find His pockets. "Seek first His Kingdom and His Righteousness and everything else will be added unto you." I have seen many who left His presence to focus only on material things. The spirit of mammon leads them to become involved in all kinds of schemes and deceitful practices. What will it be worth to a man? Therefore, God's pocket should not be our priority if we desire to be Golden Vessels. "What good will it be for someone to gain the whole world, yet forfeit their soul? Or what can anyone give in exchange for their soul?" (Matthew 16:26).

God desires us to seek His presence in everything—

even in the smallest things in life. We need His presence because only His presence can protect us from the schemes of the enemy. His presence casts out devils and allows us to reign over circumstances. When we earnestly seek God's presence, He will reward us. We will come out with great power. Our face will shine. People will see something new in your life. The glory of God will be visible and other people will see it and be blessed by it.

Moses understood the importance of God's presence when he said: "'If Your presence does not go with me, do not bring me up from here.' And God said to Moses, 'My presence will go with you, and I will give you rest'" (Exodus 33:14-15 NKJV).

Moses assured that God's presence was with him before he moved forward on his task. Many go preaching without the presence of God. Some simply focus on the wallet or other personal interests. They went ahead of God with the gift and left His presence.

God presence is the perfumes that will deal with your enemies and prosper you in life and ministry. Apostle Paul says, thanks be to God, who always leads us in triumph in Christ, and manifests through us the sweet aroma of the knowledge of Him in every place. For we are a fragrance of Christ to God among those who are being saved and among those who are perishing; to the one an aroma from death to death, to the other an aroma from life to life [2 Corinthians 2:14-16].

Seek God presence, instead of his wallet. The love of money or things of this world will take you out of His presence. Greed for money and love for the things of the world will take you out of His presence. "For the love of money produces all kinds of evil. Some people, eager for money, have wandered from the faith and have pierced themselves with many grieves" (1 Timothy 6:10).

The truth is, if you seek Him first, all the materialistic things shall then be given unto you. Cars and houses will follow, brothers and sisters will follow when you seek first His presence.

To be sure of His presence, you need to know His Word and be sensitive to the leading of the Holy Spirit. For if you make any moves without His Word it may cost you your life. The Word of God is God. He cannot do anything without His Word.

The Word is supposed to be a lamp to your feet and a light to your path; so hide it in your heart so you will not sin against God.

Joshua needed the Word to lead the people of God. Joshua 1:8 (NKJV) states: "This Book of the Law shall not depart from your mouth, but you shall meditate in it day and night, that you may observe to do according to all that is written in it. For then you will make your way prosperous, and then you will have good success." The Word makes His presence real to you.

The Holy Spirit is there to lead us in all the truth.

In John 16:13 and 15, it states: "…when He, the Spirit of truth, has come, He will guide you into all truth; for He will not speak on His own authority, but whatever He hears He will speak; and He will tell you things to come. Therefore I said that He will take of Mine and declare it to you." Being in His presence is Truth.

Seek the presence of God day and night as you develop an intimate relationship with Him.

Intimacy with God

Your intimacy with God will allow you to hear His voice clearly. Even His secrets will be revealed to you. One of the characteristics of God's Golden Vessels is that they are trusted friends of God. God has secrets and He is looking for some friends to share them with.

Surely the Lord God does nothing unless He reveals His secret to His servants the prophets (Amos 3:7).

In the Old Testament, God revealed His plan to Abraham before He destroyed Sodom and Gomorrah. That required Abraham to have an intimate relationship with Him. In the New Testament covenant, which is a better covenant, God is more willing to speak to us than we are willing to hear from Him.

If you desire to be one of God's Golden Vessels then you must become passionate to develop an intimate relationship with God, as you praise, worship, and earnestly seek His presence.

CHAPTER 9

His Name

◆

A good name is more desirable than great riches; to be esteemed is better than silver or gold (Proverbs 22:1).

THE MYSTERY BEHIND NAMES

Golden vessels discerned name. As believers we must discern names to see whether they are of God or not. A name is very significant for God and to God, even though some of us overlook it. The names of God reveal His nature to us, and likewise, the names of our adversary, the devil, reveal his character, as our opponent and his assignment against the creation of God. If you ignore it, then you will pay a high price for your ignorance. Let us briefly examine some names given to the enemy, the devil:

I. satan is the **accuser** of the brethren. Revelation 12:10 says, *Then I heard a loud voice saying in heaven, "Now salvation, and strength, and the kingdom of our God, and the power of His Christ have come, <u>for the accuser of our brethren</u>, who accused them before our God day and night, has been cast down."* This means he is there 24/7 accusing those who have inherited salvation.

II. satan is the **<u>liar and father of lies</u>**. *"You are of your father the devil, and the desires of your father you want to do. He was a murderer from the beginning, and does not stand in the truth, because there is no truth in him. When he speaks a lie, he speaks from his own resources, <u>for he is a liar</u> and the father of it"* (John 8:44).

III. satan is the **prince of darkness**. *"For we do not wrestle against flesh and blood, but against principalities, against powers, against the rulers of the darkness of this age, against spiritual hosts of wickedness in the heavenly places"* (Ephesians 6:12).

IV. satan is the **<u>adversary</u>** of God. *Be sober, be vigilant; because your adversary the devil walks about like a roaring lion, seeking whom he may devour. Resist him, steadfast in the faith, knowing that the same sufferings are experienced by your brotherhood in the world* (1 Peter 5:8-9).

The names of our enemy, satan, has been revealed to us so that we can know who we are dealing with, so that we can know his character. I have heard Christians who blamed God for everything that goes wrong in their lives. Why? They ignored the assignment carried by the enemy against their lives. The devil cannot and will not make friends with anyone. If he does, it is only to fulfill his mission to kill, steal and to destroy, or to ruin our lives.

God places a great value on names to teach us something very profound. A name can be a curse as well as a blessing. Your name can be the very reason your life is going upside down, because every time someone calls your name, they may actually calling upon something of value or something worthless; in other words, there is a spirit attached to every name—either good or bad.

Most parents will not literally call their children 'garbage', but I know people with a name that stands for garbage. For instance, "Sefatra" in Creole means garbage or trash, "good for nothing." So every time someone calls "Sefatra" or "Salopri," they are saying this person is garbage or trash, worthless or good for nothing. So the spirit that will work against that individual will make sure that person's life comes to naught. Truly, when you look at the life of such an individual you may see failure because of the spirit attached to such a name.

Abram may stand for fatherless, barrenness; but when his name was changed to Abraham, His life takes another avenue; he became father of many nations. His changed name now means father of many nations.

The Bible declares that a good name is better than precious ointment (Ecclesiastes 7:1). "A good name is rather to be chosen than great riches, and loving favour rather than silver and gold" (Proverbs 22:1).

Saul name was changed to Paul; Jacob name was changed to Israel; Abram name was changed to Abraham. Why? Because their problem was linked to their names.

A good name is better than precious ointment, gold, and silver.

"God highly exalted *the name Jesus*, and bestowed on Him the name which is above every name" (Philippians 2:9).

- Jesus became the head of the Church (Ephesians 5:23)
- He became the High Priest (Hebrews 6:20)
- He became the resurrection and the life (John 11:25)
- He became the Way, the Truth, and the Life (John 14:6)
- Jesus became the Alpha and Omega, First and Last (Revelation 22:13)
- Jesus is the Lord of lords (1 Timothy 6:15)
- Jesus became the Lion of Judah (Revelation 5:5) why? Because the given to him by God.

God dispatched his angel to tell Joseph that He should name the child Mary about to conceive the name

JESUS.

Matthew 1:20-21 An angel of the Lord appeared to him in a dream, saying, "Joseph, son of David, do not be afraid to take Mary as your wife; for the Child who has been conceived in her is of the Holy Spirit. 21"She will bear a Son; and you shall call His name **JESUS**, for He will save His people from their sins."

Pray this prayer: *I place the Name of Jesus Christ above and beyond my name and everything else I have. I cover my name with the blood of Jesus, and every evil name that has been attached to my name, I order them to leave by fire in the name of Jesus. Every bad name given to me in the dark world, leave by fire in the name of Jesus. Every curse assigned to my name, be destroyed and flushed out by the blood of Jesus. Hallelujah! Blessing is attached to my name. Healing is attached to my name. Honesty is attached to my name in the mighty name of Jesus. Amen! Amen! Amen![repeat this prayer]*

PONDER UPON THE AWESOME NAMES OF JESUS

The psalmist mentions in Psalm 63:6, "When I remember You on my bed, I meditate on You in the night watches."

The name of God reveals His nature. If He says that His name is *Jehovah Shalom*, the God of peace, then He is sharing with us that His nature is that of peace. If

He says that His name is *Jehovah Jireh*, the God who provides, then He is sharing with us that His nature is that of a provider. When we truly understand the nature of God through His names, we will not worry about what the enemy can say or will say about us.

Below is a list of the different names given to our Lord:

Jehovah Sabaoth - The Lord of Hosts: "It is as Isaiah predicted, If the Lord of hosts had not left us a seed [from which to propagate descendants], we [Israel] would have fared like Sodom and have been made like Gomorrah" (Romans 9:29).

Jehovah Jireh - The Lord our Provider: "And Abraham called the name of that place Jehovah Jireh: as it is said to this day, In the mount of the LORD it shall be seen" (Genesis 22:14).

Jehovah Nissi - The Lord is My Banner: "And Moses built an altar, and called the name of it Jehovah Nissi: For he said, 'Because the LORD hath sworn that the LORD will have war with Amalek from generation to generation'" (Exodus 17:15-16).

Jehovah Shammah - The Lord is There: "It was round about eighteen thousand measures: and the name of the city from that day shall be, The LORD is there" (Ezekiel 48:35).

Jehovah Rapha - The Lord that Heals: "And said, 'If thou wilt diligently hearken to the voice of the LORD thy God, and wilt do that which is right in his sight, and wilt give ear to his commandments, and keep all his statutes, I will put none of these diseases upon thee, which I have brought upon the Egyptians: for I am the LORD that healeth thee'" (Exodus 15:26).

"He was wounded for our transgressions, he was bruised for our iniquities: the chastisement of our peace was upon him; and with his stripes we are healed" (Isaiah 53:5).

His names should ignite the fire in us to want to know His love and His nature.

Write down three demonic situations (demon spirits) in your life you want to leave and die permanently: Say: in the name of Jesus Christ of Nazareth, I command you, [one of the names on your list below], to die and never come back again.

1. _____
2. _____
3. _____

CHAPTER 10

The Secret Room of Praise, Prayer, Dance, & Worship

◆

"Praise the Lord, all nations! Extol him, all peoples! For great is his steadfast love toward us, and the faithfulness of the Lord endures forever. Praise the Lord!" (Psalm 117:1-2)

TAP INTO PRAISE & WORSHIP

Golden vessels have a life of praise. Praise and worship is their lifestyle. A praise that is done outside of love is an abomination to the Lord. God is looking at your heart. For many people, their praise remains on a surface or bottom level where the lip is singing but the heart is saying something else. Their heart is far away from God. They sing, pray, and praise without meaning or revelation of the words that are being spoken or sung. Beloved, if there is no love in your praise or worship, it is like a clashing cymbal or like someone fighting with the wind.

God is looking at our praise and will either accept or reject it. The questions we should all be asking when we praise or worship God are: Do I mean what I say? Does my praise or my worship come from my heart? Is my heart after God or someone else? Am I just putting on a show? What is the motive of my heart when I praise? Beloved, routine praise or worship is hypocrisy. It is fleshly and carnal and it does not please God. God is looking at our heart. Is our heart saying the same thing as our mouth?

Hypocrites! Well did Isaiah prophesy about you, saying: "These people draw near to God with their mouth, And honor God with their lips, But their heart is far from Me. And in vain they worship Me" (Matthew 15:8).

Only true, heartfelt praise and worship bring glory to God. Supernatural results happened every time our praise and worship please God. When we praise God, we are expressing what He means to us. Our praise must be a sincere acknowledgment of worth, based upon our real conviction. Our praise must express how we really feel on the inside toward our Lord and Saviour Jesus Christ. When an unusual situation comes our way, we will not complain or murmur because we know our God. We know what He is capable of doing. We know who He is. Therefore, we choose to praise Him no matter what the enemy or the circumstances are saying.

Amen!

OFFER A SACRIFICIAL PRAISE TO GOD

In the Old Testament the priesthood had to offer up animal sacrifices, but we, in the New Testament, the "royal priesthood," are to offer sacrifices of praise.

> "Let us offer through Jesus a continual <u>sacrifice of praise</u> to God, proclaiming our allegiance to his name. And don't forget to do good and to share with those in need. These are the <u>sacrifices that please</u> God" (Hebrews 13:15-16).

To praise and to worship the Lord require boldness because the natural and carnal man will not praise God. Space should not a problem to praise God, no matter where you are, give Him praise, in your home, school, work, and wherever you are, praise God.

Engrave praise into your heart. "The time is coming—indeed it's here now—when true worshipers will worship the Father in spirit and in truth. The Father is looking for those who will worship him that way. For God is a Spirit, so those who worship him must worship in spirit and in truth" (John 4:24-25).

> "I will praise the name of God with a song, and will magnify Him with thanksgiving. Let the heaven and earth praise him, the seas, and

everything that moveth therein" (Psalm 69:30).

If you want to please God begin to shout praise unto Him. God loves praise. God pays more attention to your praise and worship than He does to your sacrifices and your activities in the church.

True praise and worship demand your whole being. Praise Him with all your heart, strength, and might. True praise and worship come from our inner-most being. It comes from the heart. Give Him your whole body, heart, mind, soul and will. When praising and worshiping God become top priority in our lives, we'll find no time to worry about bad news or the things of this world. Hallelujah! Praise Him.

Let's See a Few Hebrew Terms that Describe Praise and Worship:

- **Todah** means to give thanks and praise for what God is going to do.

- **Shabak** means to address the Lord with a loud tune or a loud song.

    "O praise the Lord, all ye nations: praise Him, all ye people" (Psalm 117). If you are quiet, shy, or timid, it will be difficult to get into the *shabak* praise level for in this level of praise your mouth cannot remain closed. There are times in our praise and worship when God asks for a shout of praise. Shout unto the Lord!

- **Barak** is a kind of praise meaning to kneel down

and to bless His Holy Name as an act of adoration; it shows reverence.

- **Zamar:** In this level of praise, you use instruments like the guitar, harp, piano, etc., to praise and worship God. David used music to cast out an evil spirit that came to torment King Saul. Whenever and wherever true praise and worship unto God are being done, demon spirits will be cast out; they will flee. I experience this manifestation all the time in my meetings. The sound of your praise and worship can make a destructive impact on the kingdom of darkness. So, let's praise Him.
- **Halel** means to get crazy or foolish for God. I love that one. Whenever you begin to *Halel* before God the wall of Jericho will fall flat.
- **Tehillah:** In this level there is tangible manifestation of the presence of God. God comes down and manifests Himself in the praise. Crazier for God. Everything within praise and magnify God.

INGREDIENTS TO YOUR PRAISE AND WORSHIP

Let us offer through Jesus a continual sacrifice of praise to God, proclaiming our allegiance to his name. And don't forget to do good and to share with those in need. These are the sacrifices that please God.

In Leviticus chapter 2, we read when anyone offers a grain offering to the Lord, he shall pour ***OIL*** on it, and put ***frankincense*** on it. ***No*** grain offering which you bring to the Lord shall be made with ***yeast/leaven***, for you shall burn no leaven nor any honey in any offering to the Lord made by fire.

And every offering of your grain offering you shall season with ***SALT***; you shall not allow the salt of the covenant of your God to be lacking from your grain offering. With all your offerings you shall offer ***salt.***

Whenever you offer your worship and your praise to God, you ought to be watchful of the following four ingredients:

1. **OIL** - The oil symbolizes the presence of the Holy Spirit. The Holy Ghost must be present in your life whenever you praise and worship God, otherwise you will only do tradition or religious praise and worship. The Holy Spirit must be the one directing our praise and worship unto God at all times.

2. **Frankincense** - Frankincense symbolizes the sweet smell or aroma of your offering unto God. So when the sweet smell of your true praise and worship go up some supernatural manifestation, healing, or deliverance will take place in your area. Glory to God!

3. **Yeast** - God told them not to add any yeast into their offering. Not adding yeast or leaven means that

there should not be any hypocrisy, fakeness, bitterness or resentment in your praise or worship unto God because the yeast reveals that there is dirt in that offering; it is from the lips but not from the bottom of the heart. It is like the mouth says one thing and the heart say something else. Take yeast out of your praise and worship unto God. If you hate your brothers or your sisters, then yeast has been adding to your praise and worship. If you bitter against your pastors, leaders, father or mother, then yeast has been adding to your praise and worship. Jesus told His disciples to beware of the yeast of the Pharisees; they will tell you to do something but they themselves will not do it. They are double-faced and double-minded. Repentance is the avenue for us to take out every yeast out of our lives.

4. **Salt -** Your praise and worship to God must be an everlasting covenant. Situations should not determine your level of praise and worship; you must do it anyhow. It cannot only be when things are going well, or when people are talking good about you; but even in times of need, persecution, or trials, still praise and worship God because you have a salt covenant, and a permanent alliance with Him. Amen.

The fire will test your offering of praise and worship, and if it is not real God will reject it. "The time is coming—indeed it's here now—when true worshipers will worship the Father in spirit and in truth. The Father is looking for those who will worship him that way. For

God is Spirit, so those who worship him must worship in spirit and in truth" (John 4:24-25).

TRUE PRAISE ATTRACTS ANGELS

When the enemy comes against you, use a weapon called praise. True Praise to God will put your enemy into perfect confusion. King Jehoshaphat understood clearly how to use praise to defeat his enemies. True praise attracts angelic presence. Praise bulldozes your enemies. When the enemies came to intimidate King Jehoshaphat with their bad news he called for fasting and praise unto the Lord. And the angels of the Lord waged war against the enemies. Glory be to God!

In 2 Chronicles 20:18-22 we read: "Jehoshaphat bowed down with his face to the ground, and all the people of Judah and Jerusalem fell down in worship before the LORD. Then some Levites from the Kohathites and Korahites stood up and praised the LORD, the God of Israel, with a very loud voice. After consulting the people, Jehoshaphat appointed men to sing to the LORD and to praise him for the splendor of his holiness as they went out at the head of the army, saying: 'Give thanks to the LORD, for his love endures forever.' As they began to sing and praise, the LORD set ambushes against the men of Ammon and Moab and Mount Seir who

were invading Judah, and they were defeated."

God ordained His angels to minister unto us in our daily walk with Him. But not all of us believers understand the ministry of angels. Some think angels were only in the Old Testament and not for today's time; some are afraid of angels; some think of angels as idols. But not so for God's Golden Vessels. Angels of God are waiting to serve us in every course of life. It is our word and our life in God that move them in our lives; meaning when our word is of God, Holy Angels are quick to move because they can only obey the Word of God. Angels are servants—spirits sent to care for people who will inherit salvation (Hebrews 1:14).

The angels of God are encamped around everyone who reverences God day and night to protect us. We ought to trust and believe what God says in His Word.

Psalm 34:7 states: "The angel of the Lord encampeth around about them that fear him, and delivereth them."

Angels are our servants. God placed them around us for our own benefit—not to harm us, but to lift us up from the snare and fowler of the enemy. But it requires our reverence and honor to God to allow His angels to work tirelessly for us. The Holy Angels of God are assigned to deliver us from every form of witchcraft that tries to manipulate us and work against us.

Psalm 91:11-12 declares: "For He will give His angels orders concerning you, to protect you in all your ways. They will support you with their hands so that you will not strike your foot against a stone."

Do not let anyone fool you by saying angels are not for today. If you have reverence for the Lord, His angels are there around you 24 hours a day, 7 days a week to serve and to protect you.

WARNING
NEVER WORSHIP ANGELS

If an angel asks you to worship him it is a dark angel and you need to cast it out from your presence in the Mighty Name of Jesus.

Revelation 19:10 states: "I fell at the angel feet to worship him. **But he said to me, 'Don't do that!** I am a fellow servant with you and with your brothers and sisters who hold to the testimony of Jesus. Worship God! For it is the Spirit of prophecy who bears testimony to Jesus.'"

For this study, I just want you to know that we have angels all around us, whether you see them or not. They are there. But NEVER, NEVER WORSHIP ANGELS.

Acts 27:22-26 an angel ministered to Apostle Paul who was under arrest and was being transported by ship to Italy. He and his friends, as well as the soldiers who were transporting them, were troubled by a violent wind and had lost all. Paul stood up to encourage his friends, the soldiers, and the sailors of the ship with these words: "and now I urge you to take heart, for there will be no loss of the life among you, but only of the ship. For there stood by me this night <u>an angel</u> <u>of the God</u> to whom I belong and whom I serve, saying, 'Do not be afraid, Paul; you must be brought before Caesar; and indeed God has granted you all those who sail with you.'"

Angel of the Lord ministered to Apostle Peter while he was in jail. Acts 12:7-9: "Now behold, an angel of the Lord stood by him, and a light shone in the prison; and he struck Peter on the side and raised him up, saying, 'Arise quickly!' And his chains fell off his hands. Then the angel said to him, 'Gird yourself and tie on your sandals'; and so he did. And he said to him, 'Put on your garment and follow me.'"

Angels minister to me all the time. In October of 2013 angel of God saved me from a terrible accident where my vehicle spin 360 degree, but not a hair on my head fell off. We can attract the involvement of holy angels for deliverance, healing, direction and much more.

Praise Dance Provokes Holy Angels

Is it okay to dance before the Lord? Some religious folks are very skeptical about dancing before God. Some people believe that it is unscriptural to dance before the Lord. Some get very offended when they see other people dance before the Lord. One thing I know if God is good to you, dance and don't mind who stands by you, because no one else should determine how you praise and worship the Lord of lords and King of kings. People dance in night clubs, at parties, and on sports fields, glorifying themselves or satan, but why is it that when it comes to God, people try to limit you? Beloved, if your friend does not want to praise dance before God, you get up yourself and begin to dance before God for He deserves it. Your deliverance sometimes comes about from your praise dance unto God!

King David's wife was offended when David danced before the Lord. "As the ark of the LORD was entering the City of David, Michal daughter of Saul watched from a window. And when she saw King David leaping and dancing before the LORD, she despised him in her heart" (2 Samuel 6:16).

Some church goers will be offended by your praise dance. They may even throw you out of the church like they did to the man in John chapter 9, but do not fret, just dance. "When Jesus heard that they had thrown him out (the blind man that Jesus healed), and when Jesus found him, he said, 'Do you believe in the Son of Man?' Then the man said, 'Lord, I believe,' and he worshiped Jesus."

The Pharisees and religious folks are there to stop your blessing, to stop you from glorifying God; that's their mission. They will not dance, they will not praise, they will not give and they will not worship God for themselves because they are hypocrites. But they want to stop someone else who praises God. Beware of anyone who wants to stop you from praising or glorifying God because of their religious belief or theology. Close your eyes on them and begin to praise and worship the King of kings in the Spirit and in truth.

WHY PRAISE GOD?

We praise God because it comes from the *infinite* Word of God. It is the desire of God, the Father, for every living thing to praise Him. Because He is your creator, you ought to praise Him. Hallelujah! "Let everything that has breath praise the Lord" (Psalm 150:6).

Praise allows us to continuously be filled with the Holy Ghost. "And do not be drunk with wine, in which is dissipation; but be filled with the Spirit, speaking to one another in psalms and hymns and spiritual songs, singing and making melody in your heart to the Lord, giving thanks always for all things to God the Father in the name of our Lord Jesus Christ" (Ephesians 5:18-20).

Praise God because He inhabits in the midst of Praise. "You are holy, Enthroned in the praises of Israel" (Psalm 22:3). "Great is the LORD, and greatly to be praised in the city of our God, in His holy mountain" (Psalm 48:1).

Praise the Lord for eternal life and "salvation." "For God so loved the world that He gave His only begotten Son, that whoever believes in Him should not perish but have everlasting life" (John 3:16). "But you are a chosen generation, a royal priesthood, a holy nation, His own special people, that you may proclaim the praises of Him who called you out of darkness into His marvelous light" (1 Peter 2:9).

LET YOUR CONVERSATION WITH GOD BE PRAYER OF PRAISE

Prayer of praise is loving God. It is confessing to your Heavenly Father, "Dad, I love you." Tell Him He is a good dad. "Where would I be if you were not on my side? I magnify Your Holy Name. Thank You for placing a hedge of protection around me." When you talk to God that way, your life will become stable. You will see Him as a good God when you enter His presence with such a loving attitude.

The prayer of praise says things like: "Father, I lift you above all, and you mean everything to me. Father, I am going to praise you in spite of the circumstances, for all things are in Your hands and I am Yours. You are the great I AM. I adore you as my Abba Father."

Make it your lifestyle to pray the prayer of praise. A prayer of praise is a dialogue with God. It takes different forms, and it occurs when you talk with God and God talks with you. Many of us only talk to God, but never wait to hear from Him. God wants to talk back to us when we speak to Him. Our God is not like other gods made with hands. He is not made with silver or gold. Our God speaks in the past, He speaks today, and He will continue to speak tomorrow. He is the Creator of Heaven and earth. Hallelujah!

He's not the God of the dead but of the living. You and I can talk to Him freely and expect an instant answer when we dialogue with Him. It happened in the Old Testament and it is still happening today. God speaks. Jesus Christ clearly demonstrated it with His daily conversation with God. Prayer is an indispensable to every human being.

THE TRUTHS ABOUT PRAYER

1. **Prayer is drawing near to God with a sincere Heart.** "Let us draw near to God with a sincere heart and with the full assurance that faith brings, having our hearts sprinkled to cleanse us from a guilty conscience and having our bodies washed with pure water" (Hebrews 10:22).

2. **Prayer is seeking the face of your creator.** "When thou saidst, Seek ye my face; my heart said unto thee, Thy face, LORD, will I seek" (Psalm 27:8).

3. **Prayer is lifting up your heart to God.** "Let us lift up our hearts and our hands to God in heaven"

(Lamentations 3:41).

4. **Prayer is pouring out your heart to God.** "Trust in him at all times, you people; pour out your hearts to him, for God is our refuge" (Psalm 62:8).

THE PRAYER LIFE OF OUR LORD JESUS CHRIST

Prayer was spiritual food in the life of our Lord Jesus Christ:

Jesus Christ made prayer to His Heavenly Father a priority. "He prayed any time of the day or night: One of those days Jesus went out to a mountainside to pray, and spent the night praying to God. When morning came, he called his disciples to him and chose twelve of them" (Luke 6:12-13).

Prayer took priority over food. "Meanwhile his disciples urged him, 'Rabbi, eat something.' But he said to them, 'I have food to eat that you know nothing about'" (John 4:31-32).

At His baptism: "As he was praying, heaven was opened and the Holy Spirit descended on him in bodily form like a dove. And a voice came from heaven: 'You are my Son, whom I love; with you I am well pleased.'" (Luke 3:21-22)

Jesus prayed before the choosing of His disciples

(as Luke 6:12-13 above showed us). Before we choose a business partner or someone to be our mate or partner in ministry, we must invest time in prayer to be sure of God's approval.

He prayed before and after the feeding of the 5,000. "Taking the five loaves and the two fish and looking up to heaven, he gave thanks and broke the loaves. Then he gave them to the disciples, and the disciples gave them to the people. After he had dismissed them, he went up on a mountainside by himself to *pray*. Later that night, he was there alone" (Matthew 14:19-23).

He was in prayer before Peter received the revelation of who He is. "Once when Jesus was praying in private and His disciples were with him, he asked them, 'Who do the crowds say I am?'" (Luke 9:18).

He prayed at the grave of Lazarus. "So they took away the stone. Then Jesus looked up and said, 'Father, I thank you that you have heard me. I knew that you always hear me, but I said this for the benefit of the people standing here, that they may believe that you sent me'" (John 11:41-42).

If prayer was important to Jesus, the only begotten Son of God, why are we not praying? Why isn't there any answer to our prayers? My friend, if your prayer life is dead or cold, I strongly believe that there is a problem somewhere that needs close attention. We better ask the Comforter, the Holy Spirit, to teach us how to pray. The Holy Spirit came to teach us the way of God. He empowers us to pray effectively for He came to lead us into all truth.

CHAPTER 11

A Trustworthy Companion

◆

"There is a friend who sticks closer than a brother" (Proverbs 18:24).

Golden vessels have a trustworthy companion. There is a friend who sticks closer than a brother and that friend is the Holy Spirit of God. I spent more than fourteen years in church, yet I did not know this vital and trustworthy companion. All I knew about Him was that I received Him as a seal till the day of redemption (Ephesians 1:13).

I didn't know I could talk to him, or whether or not He could teach me or correct me. But when I came across John 14:26 which clearly says, "the Advocate, the Holy Spirit, whom the Father will send in my name, will teach you all things and will remind you of everything I have said to you," I was amazed.

In John 16:7 Jesus declared, it is for our good that He is going away. Unless He went away, the Advocate would not come to us; but because He went, He sent the Holy Spirit to us.

I discovered that living in this world without the leading and the guidance of this Companion, the Holy Spirit, is not only miserable, but it is a life of struggling, fearful, desperation and powerlessness. Jesus Christ, Himself, did nothing without the Holy Spirit. I visit many churches and meet people who called themselves Christian, yet, they do not believe in the power of the Holy Spirit. How can you not believe in the power of the Holy Spirit? If Jesus Christ, the Son of the Most High God, needed the Holy Spirit to function on earth, then what about us? If you don't need Him, I do. Truly, anything we do without the leading of the Holy Spirit is flesh. The flesh cannot please God; only the Holy Spirit can.

I want to briefly mention that the Holy Spirit is not oil. He is not a wind. He is not a fire. He is not a cloud. He is not a dove. He is not a handkerchief. These are only medium the Holy Spirit uses. *The Holy Spirit is the third person of the Godhead.* He is the Teacher. He is the Comforter. He came to reveal Jesus Christ to all humanity. He is exactly like Jesus. He is not less than the Father, nor is He less than Jesus. He is one with God the Father and God the Son. Jesus knew the importance of the Holy Spirit. He understood this glorious person and He knew His personality well. That was the reason He could trust Him, and before He ever came to earth to take upon Himself the form of man, He committed Himself to the working of the Holy Spirit. That is why during the course of His ministry on earth, He never failed.

"God anointed Jesus of Nazareth with the Holy Spirit and power, and he went around doing good and healing all who were under the power of the devil, because God was with him" (Acts 10:38).

God demonstrated to us that we have to depend also on the voice and the leading of the Holy Spirit to do the will of God the Father. If you are looking for a trustworthy companion, seek the Holy Spirit. He is the only One who can lead you in the right path. He is trustworthy. He will never betray you. He will never forsake you. He will never give up on you. He is there to reveal to you even the deepest secrets and things of God.

Jesus said: "I will ask the Father, and he will give you another Advocate, who will never leave you. He is the Holy Spirit, who leads into all truth. It isn't looking for him and doesn't recognize him. But you know him, because he lives with you now and later will be in you" (John 14:16-17).

If you deny the Holy Spirit, you deny God also. We get into trouble because we do not trust the voice of the Holy Spirit. And sometimes we put more confidence in the saying of men rather than focusing on what the Holy Spirit is telling us to do.

The Holy Spirit is vital to all of God's Golden Vessels because they cannot please God without the Holy Spirit. Holy Spirit will defend you. I don't talk much. People knew me as a very quiet boy even when I was in primary school. I learned to keep silence even when people said wrong thing about me or lied on me. I just leave it to the Holy Spirit to avenge or defend me. If you give Holy Spirit a change to defend you, He uses time to reveal truths.

"Those who are led by the Spirit of God are Sons of God. For as many as are led by the Spirit of God, these are sons of God" (Romans 8:14).

Every powerful man and woman of God in the Bible functioned under the leading of the Holy Spirit. Without Him they were powerless. If our life is dry and meaningless today, it is because we are not being led by the Holy Spirit. The Holy Spirit is our pilot. He is right by our side to lead us into all truths, to strengthen us, etc. The Old Testament believers had the Holy Spirit occasionally, but today, we have the Holy Spirit 24 hours a day and 7 days a week. And He will be with us forever.

When Jesus walked upon this earth, He did not heal sick bodies, cast out devils, or raise the dead in His own strength. A million times No! It was the Holy Spirit who did those things through Him.

Just as Jesus needed the help of the Holy Spirit to carry out the intentional will of God, likewise, we need the help of the Holy Spirit to walk in the power of God. It is not God's fault when we walk powerless because we have the Holy Spirit with us; we just need to employ His help. The Holy Spirit comes to live in you to make you His dwelling.

"And I will pray the Father and He shall give you another Comforter, that He may abide with you forever, even the Spirit of truth, whom the world cannot receive because it seeth him not, neither knoweth Him: but ye know him for he dwelled with you, and shall be in you" (John 14:16-17).

Pray this Prayer: I want to be filled with the Holy Spirit. Holy Spirit, take your full place on the throne of my life. Fill me with yourself as the Word of God commanded me to be filled. As an expression of faith, I thank You, Father God, for taking control of my life and for filling me with the Holy Spirit. I am filled with the Holy Ghost from the top of my head to the soles of my feet in the name of Jesus. Amen and amen!

CHAPTER 12

Faithful Servants Become Great Leaders

◆

"Serve one another in love" (Galatians 5:13).

Golden vessels understand the principle of a faithful servant for a faithful servant will become great leader. There are some misconceptions about servant-hood. Some people only want other people to serve them while they will not serve others. That is a type of manipulation. Being a servant does not mean that you are less than others. It does not mean you are uneducated, or that you are blind or poor. Having a servant's spirit is a character trait given by God. He Himself served even His own creation.

In Matthew 20:26-27, we read, "Whoever wants to be a leader among you must be your servant, and whoever wants to be first among you must become your slave. That's the secret of becoming a great leader in the kingdom of God."

Serving others is the nature of God's Golden Vessels. Jesus said, "I came to serve and not to be served."

We were saved to serve. Without the attitude of servant-hood, it will be difficult to be used as a vessel of honor in the hands of God. God Himself served us. He served Adam and Eve in the garden after they sinned against Him; He made clothes for them to cover their shame and their nakedness.

Not everyone grasps the principle of serving, but anyone anticipating to becoming great in the kingdom of God must learn to serve others and do it with love.

The Bible declares that "If anyone serves, he should do it with the strength God provides, so that in all things God may be praised through Jesus Christ" (1 Peter 4:11).

When we look at successful men and women of God in the Bible, we see that their achievements are because of the service they gave to others. When we serve others, we position ourselves for uncommon promotion. God will promote us, and we will see the manifestation of His blessing upon us when we dedicate our lives to serve others. Not everyone will accept our services. Some will mock you, some will despise you, some will try to kill you; but in the midst of it all, if you are faithful, God will lift you up.

Samuel served and became a Great Leader.

The Prophet Samuel served in the house of God at a very young age, and because of his faithfulness in serving God and the priest, Eli, God elevated him to a position of honor. "And all Israel from Dan to Beersheba knew that Samuel had been established as a prophet of the LORD" (1 Samuel 3:20).

He served as a priest... "Samuel took a suckling lamb and offered it as a whole burnt offering to the LORD. Then Samuel cried out to the LORD for Israel, and the LORD answered him. Now as Samuel was offering up the burnt offering, the Philistines drew near to battle against Israel. But the LORD thundered with a loud thunder upon the Philistines that day, and so confused them that they were overcome before Israel" (1 Samuel 7:9-10).

He served as judge over the people of God... "Samuel judged Israel all the days of his life. He went from year to year on a circuit to Bethel, Gilgal, and Mizpah, and judged Israel in all those places. But he always returned to Ramah his hometown. There he judged Israel, and there he built an altar to the LORD" (1 Samuel 7:15-17). "Samuel grew, and the LORD was with him and God let none of Samuel's words fall to the ground" (1 Samuel 3:19). God honored every word spoken by Samuel, His faithful servant.

King David served and became a great King

He served as a shepherd boy in the house of his

father. He served King Saul for many years. Whatever the king asked him to do, he did it. In 1 Samuel 18:5, we read: "Whatever Saul sent him to do, David did it so successfully that Saul gave him a high rank in the army. This pleased all the people, and Saul's officers as well."

David's faithfulness placed him in a position to be promoted. God took him from tending sheep in the pasture and selected him to be king over His people. David served the people of God for over thirty years.

God testified of David, and said: "I have found David the son of Jesse, a man after My own heart, who will do all My will" (Acts 13:22). David was a faithful servant.

Jesus Christ served us and became the Savior and Lord of the whole world.

"Just as the Son of Man did not come to be served, but to serve, and to give his life as a ransom for many" (Matthew 20:28).

Jesus served the little ones when He laid His hands on them and blessed them. He washed the feet of His disciples. He fed over 5000 hungry folks to demonstrate the love and the compassion He had for them. True servants serve and do not focus on being served. Jesus was given the name that is above every name. Why? Because He has a heart to serve us. It is His nature.

Philippians 2:5-11 tells us, "Jesus who, being in the form of God, did not consider it robbery to be equal with God, but made Himself of no reputation, taking the form of a bondservant, and coming in the likeness of men. And being found in appearance as a man, He humbled Himself and became obedient to the point of death, even the death of the cross. Therefore God also has highly exalted Him and given Him the name which is above every name, that at the name of Jesus every knee should bow, of those in heaven, and of those on earth, and of those under the earth, and that every tongue should confess that Jesus Christ is Lord, to the glory of God the Father."

Even though He was the King of kings, He served the least of His nation. What about us? Are you serving others?

God elevated Jesus Christ after He served humanity. Jesus served us faithfully till His death on the cross. Are you a true servant of the Lord? Do you want to become great in the kingdom of God? If so, then serve others, even the least among you, and do it with sincere love. Anyone who desires to be used by God as a Golden Vessel must first learn to serve.

CHAPTER 13

Fear Not, Your Enemies Have Been Defeated

◆

Do not fear of your enemies for they are only bread for you. They have no protection, their protection has been removed from them because the Lord is with us, do not fear of them.

Golden vessels are not afraid of the enemy for 2000 years ago the enemy has been defeated by Jesus. The enemy may uses terror and dread to keep people in bondages. He oppresses people to fear the economy, to be afraid of tomorrow, to worry about they are going to eat and so on. But beloved, remember that our God is against the dread of the enemy. Two thousand years ago, Jesus disarmed the rulers and authorities. Jesus made a public display of satan and all his hosts, He shamed the enemy. On the cross He triumphed over them. Today, He gives us peace instead of worry. He gives us joy instead of anxiety. With that said, you and I can go and walk over the tricks of the enemy no matter how they come in.

For the Lord has not given a spirit of fear but of power. Jesus said, go and heal the sick, cast out devils, etc. This command was given to people who were on His side, meaning, His disciples, His pupils, His believers.

It is very dangerous to go out and ignoring the One who sent you and the One who is with you. 1 John 4:4 says, "He who is in you is greater than he who is in the world." "If God is for me who can be against me" (Romans 8:31).

The Prophet Elisha knew who was in him; he knew that the Great "I AM" was on the inside of him and so he rested. "And when the servant of the man of God arose early and went out, there was an army, surrounding the city with horses and chariots. And his servant said to him, 'Alas, my master! What shall we do?' He answered, 'Do not fear, for those who are with us are more than those who are with them.' And Elisha prayed, and said, 'Lord, I pray, open his eyes that he may see.' Then the Lord opened the eyes of the young man, and he saw. And behold, the mountain was full of horses and chariots of fire all around Elisha."

I have seen many Christians, precious children of God that go through many things in life, why? The devil presses them down to the ground and they agree to stay there. They go through sufferings with various diseases; They are oppressed by demonic spirits. Although God has given them the authority and power over these demons, they still do not know how to keep their feet upon the necks of the enemy.

Beloved, the authority and dominion that we have been given as believers are our identification; they have set us apart from the children of darkness. When we speak our words ruled over the words or incantations of the enemies. The same authority that Jesus our Rabbi functioned with while on earth, is the same authority He left us. In Him we can do all things. Why? Because if we abide in Him He abides in us (John 15:4). Wow! "Greater is He who is in us than he who is in the world" (1 John 4:4). He has given us the key to the kingdom. He revealed to us even the deep secret things of the Spirit that the world does not know.

The Apostle Paul understood the One who sent him and the One who was with him. He declared, 'when I came to you I did not come with persuasive speech, or wisdom of men, but I came with demonstration of the power of the Holy Ghost. When God is for and with me, who can be against me?'

It is upsetting to see a child of God live a powerless or defeated life. Why? Jesus Christ had invested all He has in us to live a victorious life and a life of dominion over the power of the enemy? **My people are perished because of lack of knowledge. Jesus** said, "Behold, I give you the authority to trample on serpents and scorpions, and over all the power of the enemy, and nothing shall by any means hurt you" (Luke 10:19). "And

I give you the keys of the kingdom of heaven, and whatever you bind on earth will be bound in heaven, and whatever you loose on earth will be loosed in heaven" (Matthew 16:19). He also said, "You can be sure that I will be with you always. I will continue with you until the end of the world" (Matthew 28:20b).

God cannot lie. Whatever He says, it is Yes and Amen! His Word will only work for those who take it and put it into practice—not just a hearer, but one who will hide the Word in his heart. It is time to declare, "I can do all things through Christ who gives me power and authority." Jesus has already fought and won the battle against the devil for us, and He put us inside Himself so that we can walk in the same glorious and victorious life that He walked in over two thousand years ago.

Jesus disarmed all evil powers and authorities, and made openly a public spectacle of them so that you and I won't have to be afraid of them. We can walk in their face and say boldly, "I rebuke you, satan, in the name of Jesus." Glory be to God!

"Having wiped out the handwriting of requirements that was against us, which was contrary to us. And He has taken it out of the way, having nailed it to the cross. And having disarmed the powers and authorities, he made a public spectacle of them, triumphing over them by the cross" (Colossians 2:14-15). Fear not for Jesus Christ defeated all your enemies two thousand years ago. Go on in this journey of your life and ministry and keep on walking from one step of victory to another step of victory in Jesus name.

CHAPTER 14

Walk in the Power of His Might

♦

In Psalm 8:6 the Bible declares that God has given us dominion over the works of His hands; He has put all things under our feet. Why should we live below the level of life that God intentionally planned for us to live?

Golden vessels walk in power and dominion. From the beginning of creation we were made to walk in dominion over every creeping and living thing. In other words, God wants us to have complete dominion over every situation in life. It does not matter of your skin color, gender, race—black or white, God created you to step up from being a clay, wooden, or silver vessel to be a Golden Vessel where He can use you for honorable works. He called us to walk in great power of the Holy Spirit—power to keep the devil upside down, power to change our situation. We have been given power to destroy witchcraft manipulation and power to reverse the works of darkness in our lives.

That dominion and power are available to every man or woman whom God created. God shows no favoritism. Come to Him with a humble heart and receive it by faith and start walking in it.

ORDINARY PEOPLE WHO WALKED IN THE POWER AND DOMINION OF HIS MIGHT

(1) **Apostle Paul was transformed from a murderer to a Golden Vessel and he walked in power.** He did unusual signs and wonders and miracles throughout his ministry. He laid his hands on those who believed; the Holy Spirit came on them, and they spoke in other tongues and prophesied (Acts 19:6).

(2) **Stephen walked in the power of His Might.** Acts 6:8 declares that he was a man full of God's grace and power who performed great wonders and signs among the people.

(3) **Philip walked in the power of His Might.** He went to the city of Samaria and told the people there about the Messiah. Crowds listened intently to Philip because they were eager to hear his message and see the miraculous signs he did. Many evil spirits were

cast out, screaming as they left their victims. And many who had been paralyzed or lame were healed. So there was great joy in that city (Acts 8:4-8).

These were men and women of God, just like you and me.

ARE YOU WALKING IN THE POWER OF HIS MIGHT?

To walk in the power of the Holy Spirit requires submission to the Holy Spirit, trusting Him, and obedience to the Word of God. As you position yourself in a place of submission and yielding to the voice of the Holy Spirit, then God will confirm your message with great signs and wonders.

Apostle Paul said: "…My message and my preaching were not with wise and persuasive words, but with a demonstration of the Spirit's <u>power</u>."

Jesus said: "I have given you <u>authority</u> over all the <u>power</u> of the enemy, and you can walk among snakes and scorpions and crush them. Nothing will injure you" (Luke 10:19 NLT).

Many of us cannot see the manifestation of the power of God in our lives because of fear, doubt, unbelief, and a lack of knowledge of the word of God. Some of us are afraid of the enemy even though the Scriptures clearly state that God does not give us a spirit of fear. He gave us power, love, and of sound-mind (2 Timothy 1:7). The word of God is God. What He said is what He mean, therefore we trust the word and let it work for us.

Mark 16:15-18 states: "Jesus said to them, 'Go into all the world and preach the gospel to every creature. And these signs will follow those who believe: In My name they will cast out devils, they will speak with new tongues, they will take up serpents, and if they drink anything deadly it will by no means hurt them.'"

He told us not to be afraid. When we let go of doubt and unbelief in our hearts and simply trust and obey Him, then nothing by any means will hurt or stop us. This is the Word of the Lord. If you believe it, you will see its manifestation. I refuse to act as though the Word of God is like a fairytale.

The Word of God declares clearly that signs would follow those who are born again; there is no favoritism in this. You and I simply need to put our trust in the Word of our Lord and Savior Jesus Christ. Each believer is supposed to be a sign or an advertisement and an evidence of the testimony of our Lord Jesus Christ.

I am willing. I am willing to step up into the deepest things of God to see the manifestation of His Word in my life. Are you willing? Jesus is very clear on where we should go and what we should do. He said, "In My name they will <u>cast out demons</u>; they will speak with <u>new tongues</u>; they will <u>take up serpents</u>; and if they drink anything deadly, it will by no means hurt them; they will lay hands on the sick, and they will recover." Not with your own knowledge or experience, but in the powerful name of Jesus Christ! It works, beloved.

Even regarding miracles, one thing people fail to grasp is that miracles, signs, and wonders were given to us by God as evidence of who we are representing. Jesus walked with signs and wonders everywhere He went. There was always a great demonstration of the power of God in His life. To give credibility for the Gospel that we are preaching, He made available signs and wonders. He confirms the message we preach and teach with signs and wonders. In other words, they validated Jesus' message as truth. Believe it or not, beloved, we greatly need signs, wonders, and miracles to distinguish whose God is God. Prophet Elijah proved his God was the true God with a sign—fire—to close the mouths of the false prophets of Baal. If you are a believer, you need Mark 16:17-18 to follow your life.

Let's me share with you few nuggets about walking in the power of His Might:

#1 KEEP THE WORD INSTEAD OF TRADITION

We must keep His word not our tradition. In Mark 7:8-9, it states: "people are Neglecting the commandment of God to hold to the tradition of men."

Jesus was also saying to them, "You are experts at setting aside the commandment of God in order to keep your tradition."

Tradition is man's ways of doing things. Tradition keeps people under bondage. Tradition would rather you die instead of doing what God is asking. Tradition is one thing that made the Word of God ineffective in the lives of many believers. People want to do things their way instead of God's way.

Jesus said, "<u>Lay hands</u> on the sick, and they will recover"; but many of us say, "Oh, no! That's not for today. What if the person does not get healed?" When we talk that way, we are walking in disobedience. He said lay your hands. All you have to say is "Yes, Sir." Well, because of our disobedience many people die before their time. Unless we are obedient to the Lord's command, we will not see the sick recover. In a particular crusade I prayed for a lady with a tumor in the brain, and God supernaturally healed her. You may ask, how did that happened? I don't know, but because I was obedient and laid my hand, God did the miracle. Glory to God.

"Is any sick among you? (The Word tells us what to do.) Let him (the sick person) call for the elders of the church; and let them <u>pray</u> over him, <u>anointing</u> him <u>with oil</u> in the name of the Lord: And the prayer of faith shall save the sick, and the Lord shall raise him up; and if he have committed sins, they shall be forgiven him"

(James 5:13-15).

> "Don't just listen to God's Word. You must do what it says, otherwise, you are only fooling yourselves; for if you listen to the Word and don't obey, it is like glancing at your face in a mirror. You see yourself, walk away, and forget what you looked like. But if you look carefully into the perfect law that sets you free, and if you do what it says and don't forget what you heard, then God will bless you for doing it" (James 1:22-25).

#2 Delight in the Word, not our own understanding

We must delight in His word. Delight means great joy or extreme pleasure. Man's delight is in the law; not just the law of Moses, but all the ways of God. Our delight should be in the Holy Bible, that is, in what God asks or requires of us. We should have a love and a deep passion to know and to understand the Word of God such that we look forward to seeing what the Word has to say about our lives, our situations, our finances, our marriages, and so forth. We need to be excited about understanding the ways of God. Watch closely for the Word of God because it will not return to Him without performing the exact thing He sent it to do, said the Lord Almighty God. Wow! I am excited about it. I yearn to see His Word fulfilled in my life for the Word of God endures eternally.

#3 There is no Ending to His Word

We must understand that the word of the Lord has no end. We can trust the Word of God because it is eternal. Whatever He says, you can say, "YES", I believe Him.' If you have that expectation, you will see the miraculous side of God manifest in your very own life.

"Your eternal word, O LORD, stands firm in heaven" (Psalm 119:89). "I will never forget Your Words, [how can I?] for it is by them You have quickened me (granted me life)" (Psalm 119:93). "Oh, how love I Your word! It is my meditation all the day."

Luke 21:33 declares: "Heaven and earth will pass away, but <u>My words</u> will by <u>no means pass away</u>. *All flesh is as grass, and all the glory of man as the flower of the grass. The grass withers, and its flower falls away, <u>but the word of the LORD endures forever</u>*" (1 Peter 1:24-25).

"God *is* not a man, that He should lie, Nor a son of man, that He should repent. Has He said, and will He not do? Or has He spoken, and will He not make it good?" (Numbers 23:19).

If you and I have that level of expectation knowing that the Word of God remains eternally and God cannot separate Himself from His Word, then we'll experience His power without measure.

#4 The Word is a Sword, not a fraud

We must use the word as a sword to cut off the

necks of the enemy. God's Golden Vessels use the Sword of the Spirit to fight the enemy, satan. Your head, hands, legs, nor your beautiful face will not and cannot effectively fight the enemy. You will lose the battle if you depend on these things. You need ***the Sword of the Spirit*** which is ***the Word of God*** to fight the deceptive tricks or schemes of the devil.

It is very sad to see, but a lot of folks all around the world are not even aware that there is a spiritual fight. If something happens to them, they immediately say, 'I got hurt; it is painful.' They are vulnerable. Many in our society have some idea that satan exists or wicked spirits exist, but their understanding of satan is confused and distorted because they have been fooled into believing the popular images of satan. For instance, they may see satan as someone with a big tooth, red, long, filthy hair, an ugly face and so on. But satan has them fooled so much so that he has the help of human beings to operate his schemes. They do not see satan for the cruel being he really is.

The Bible declares that the battle is not carnal; it is not flesh and blood, but spiritual. We are fighting against principalities, powers, rulers of the darkness of this age, and spiritual hosts of wickedness in the heavenly places; therefore, we cannot ignore the deceiving tricks of the enemy, satan.

How did Jesus deal with the devil in His earthly ministry? When satan tempted Him, He simply stood

His ground and used the **Sword of the Spirit, the Word of God**. In every temptation, He declared: "It is written."

> **Jesus said to the devil, "You shall not tempt the LORD your God."** Again, the devil took Him up on an exceedingly high mountain, and showed Him all the kingdoms of the world and their glory. And he said to Him, "All these things I will give You if You will fall down and worship me." Then Jesus said to him, "Away with you, Satan! For **it is written**, *'You shall worship the LORD your God, and Him only you shall serve'*" (Matthew 4:7-10).

Jesus, Himself, quoted the Word of God, using it as a sword against satan. Why? The words are spirit and life. In John 6:63 it reads, "the Spirit alone gives eternal life. Human effort accomplishes nothing. And the very words I have spoken to you are spirit and life."

From the very beginning of creation God used the Word. Why? Because words are very powerful. Every time a word is spoken there is an angel or angels who take it to fulfill it. The angel can be either Holy angels or unholy angels. The Word of God accompanies the Holy angels and evil words accompany dark angels.

God spoke a word. He said, "Let there be light," and there was light. And God saw that the light was good. Then he separated the light from the darkness. God called the light "day" and the darkness "night." And evening passed and morning came, marking the first day. Then God said, "Let there be a space between the waters, to separate the waters of the heavens from the waters of the earth." And that is what happened. God made this space to separate the waters of the earth from the waters of the heavens. God called the space "sky." And evening passed and morning came, marking the second day (Genesis 1).

God spoke a word and that word went out to do exactly what God said.

Jesus did not use any other way to fight; He defeated the devil with *faith in the Word of God*. How do you fight the devil? Are you using the Word of God or something else? God gave us His Word as an undefeated weapon to fight the enemy. God's Word is anointed. The Sword of the Spirit, the Word of God, breaks the yoke of bondage. Why are you not using the Word?

One thing about the Golden Vessels is that they have a passion for praying the Word, singing the Word, praising, worshiping and *living the Word*. "If you **abide** in Me, and My **words abide** in you, you will ask what you desire, and it shall be done for you" (John 15:7).

Abiding in the Word will place you in that level of honor or as a Golden Vessel in the hands of God.

DON'T WORRY ABOUT THE GOSSIPERS AND THE SLANDERERS

People will talk evil about you once you are in the hand of God as His God's Golden Vessels. When you begin to walk in dominion and in the power of the Holy Spirit, the devil will use people to plot against you. The gossipers will talk. The slanders will talk but fear not for God is with you. They will be resentful of you and call you names like false pastor, fake prophet, crazy, demon possessed, etc. But do not focus on them, because these are just stumbling blocks to stop you from doing the will of God. They plotted and said all kinds of evil things against all the prophets of God and even against Jesus Christ our Lord and Savior. They called Him names. They said He was out of His mind.

They said, "He is possessed by Beelzebul," and "He casts out the demons by the ruler of the demons" (Mark 3:22). But He remained faithful to His Father. If men say wrong things about you, if they persecute you because you are a Christian, then you are blessed, because the wonderful Spirit, the Spirit of God, is with you (1 Peter 4:14).

> **Surely He shall deliver you from the snare of the fowler, *And* from the perilous pestilence. He shall cover you with His feathers, And under His wings you shall take refuge; His truth *shall be your* shield and buckler. A thousand may fall at your side, And ten thousand at your right hand; *But* it shall not come near you. Only with your eyes shall you look, And see the reward of the wicked. Because you have made the LORD, *who is* my refuge, *Even* the Most High, your dwelling place (Psalms 91).**

I dare you to believe the Word of God, trust the Word of God, and delight yourself entirely in the Word of God and surely you will see great manifestations of His power over your life and ministry because whatever God says, He will do it.

Prayer point: (1) I will not live a powerless Christian life in Jesus' Name. (2) No matter what comes my way I will overcome it in the Name of Jesus Christ of Nazareth. (3) I will eat the Word of God day and night. I will meditate on it without ceasing so that I can please my God in every possible way in Jesus' name. Amen!

CHAPTER 15

Barricades in Life

◆

For the days will come upon you, when your enemies will set up a barricade around you and surround you and hem you in on every side (Luke 19:43).

Be alert and be of a sober mind. Your enemy, the devil, prowls around like a roaring lion looking for someone to devour.

Lest Satan should get an advantage of us: for we are not ignorant of his devices. Golden vessels are not ignorant of satan' schemes. Some people are unable to reach their golden level in life because of evil barricades. The devil assigned his agents to work days and nights as barricades to cut off the people of God from their holy walk with God. They try to get our focus off the things of God and pull us from the way of truth and lead us into deception and lies!

In Jeremiah 5:26-27, we read, "For among My people are found wicked men; They lie in wait as one who sets snares; They set a trap; They catch men. As a cage is full of birds, So their houses are full of deceit. Therefore they have become great and grown rich."

Prayer: I prophesy against every evil tree cutter assigned against your life today and I commend them to leave your life and to disappear forever in the name of Jesus.

This is what the word of God is saying In Psalm 1:3: "He shall be like a tree planted by the rivers of water, that brings forth its fruit in its season, whose leaf also shall not wither; and whatever he does shall prosper."

The above verse declares a powerful truth about us sons and daughters of God. Our lives are to be like trees planted by the stream of water, bringing its fruit in every season, never drying out. But our enemies who know this assign their agents or hosts to cut our lives off; these devils are there to cut our lives off from the joy of the Lord—to cut us away from our peace, our wealth, our health, and so forth.

In Mark 8, we read about a man who saw everyone like trees. If Jesus would let that man go on the street with that mindset, he would cut off the legs of everyone he finds in his way. Why? He saw people contrary to the way God saw them. When you underestimate or look down at God's image you do the same thing as that man who saw everyone like trees.

The wicked kill and destroy people because they see everyone contrary to the way God sees us. They see people like trees, or like chickens, or like goats, or like rams. They do not see you the way God sees you, and so they make their way to destroy the very thing God created. That is why if one touch is not enough we need another touch from the Lord so that we can see clearly the same way with God.

> **Then Jesus came to Bethsaida; and they brought a blind man to Him, and begged Him to touch him. So He took the blind man by the hand and led him out of the town. And when He had spit on his eyes and put His hands on him, He asked him if he saw anything. And he looked up and said, "<u>I see men like trees, walking</u>." Then He put His hands on his eyes again and made him look up. And he was restored and saw everyone clearly (Mark 8:22-24).**

The enemy manipulates people and uses them as barricade to destroy the work of God in our lives. satan oppressed people to carry on his evil assignments. We need to understand the schemes of the enemy and destroy them right away. Jesus Christ was manifested in the world to destroy the works of satan in our lives. And so as Golden Vessels our assignment is to do the same, destroy the works of satan in the name of Jesus.

2 Corinthians 2:11 states "...we are not ignorant of satan's schemes or devices," meaning we ought to know satan's plans against our lives, finances, health, etc. If we refuse to destroy the devil's plans over our lives, he will destroy us. In this new covenant we do not fight against flesh and blood but against principalities, evil spirits etc. Do not fight your brother and sister, but fight the devil, deal with the demon spirits and it shall be well with you.

In John 10:10, Jesus told us clearly the purpose of satan on earth: he came to steal, kill and destroy.

satan is the driver behind every barricade in our lives. He uses people to carry his evil assignments:

Jezebel was a barricade for the people of God, till the man of God, Jehu, came and removed her. Second Kings 9:32 states: "And he looked up at the window, and said, 'Who is on my side? Who?' So two or three eunuchs looked out at him. Then he said, 'Throw Jezebel down.' So they threw her down, and some of her blood spattered on the wall and on the horses; and he trampled her underfoot."

Judas Iscariot was a barricade to the Gospel of our Lord Jesus till he hanged himself. He was an evil tree cutter for Jesus. He was hired by satan to betray Jesus.

Sanballat and Tobiah were barricades to Nehemiah and the people of God till God dealt with them.

Saul of Tarsus was a barricade to the new believers until Jesus knocked him off his horse (Acts 9:4).

The devil assigns many wicked people to cut Christians off from their streams of blessings. Your life was supposed to prosper like a tree planted by a stream of water, but you have seen the opposite: drought, failure, disappointment, etc. Many times the reason you are not bearing fruit is because of the work of the tree cutters in your life!

But I am here to tell you, even if they have cut your finances down, your health down, your family down, your marriage down, or your ministry down, Jesus Christ still has the power to bring it back to life. There is still hope for you as a tree planted by the stream of water. Yield yourself unto Him, the giver of life. For Jesus Christ is the same yesterday, today and forever (Hebrews 13:8).

For there is hope for a tree,
    If it is cut down, that it will sprout again,
    And that its tender shoots will not cease.
Though its root may grow old in the earth,
    And its stump may die in the ground,
Yet at the scent of water it will bud
    And bring forth branches like a plant (Job 14:7-9).

Prayer Points: (1) Every evil assignment against my life be nullified in the name of Jesus Christ of Nazareth. (2) Every tree cutter making it their business to torment my life, die in the Name of Jesus. (3) Every tree altar built to torment my destiny be destroyed by fire in the name of Jesus!

CHAPTER 16

The Purpose of the Enemy Revealed

◆

In John 10:10 we read, the thief comes only to steal, kill, and destroy.

The devil speaks against the people of God every day. The thief does not come to make friends with anybody; He only comes to steal, to kill, and to destroy. Witches and voodoo priests prophesy curses over believers on a daily basis. We cannot play with the devil. His ministries are to divert the plan of God over our life as a man or woman of God. His agents talk negatively daily against us. They enchant evil things against our lives, against our families, against our wealth, etc., and it is my responsibility and yours to stand upon the Word of the Lord and prophesy good things over our lives.

In Psalm 55:2-3, 9-10, we read, "Hear me and answer me. My thoughts trouble me and I am distraught because of what my enemy is saying, because of the threats of the wicked; for they bring down suffering on me and assail me in their anger. Lord, confuse the wicked, confound their words, for I see violence and strife in the city. Day and night they prowl about on its walls; malice and abuse are within it."

The devil and all its hosts are on a mission to change God's purpose over your life and over the entire humanity. He brings disorder and discord into the world. When God says life, it says death. When God says prosperity, the devil says poverty. When God says moving forward, it say moving backward. When God says healing, it say sickness. You see, the devil comes to bring confusion in the divine order of God's establishment. We must stand up with God and His holy hosts to destroy the works of darkness in our lives and in the lives of others.

SKEPTICS DON'T BELIEVE DEMONS EXIST!

It is very sad to say, but there are people right in the house of God who walk around believing the lie that demons or evil spirits don't exist. Some say demon is a fairytale. No wonder why the bible say my people are perished because of the lack of knowledge. God's Golden Vessels hate demons spirits so much that they reverse their activities and cast them out on a daily basis.

satan and all its hosts are our enemies. They are the real enemies behind all our bad situations and chaos of life. For we wrestle not against flesh and blood, but against principalities, against powers, against the rulers of the darkness of this world, against spiritual wickedness in high places (Ephesians 6:12).

Listen to what the Word says about unclean spirits, demons, or evil spirits:

> "When an impure spirit comes out of a person, it goes through arid places seeking rest and does not find it. Then it says, 'I will return to the house I left.' When it arrives, it finds the house unoccupied, swept clean and put in order. Then it goes and takes with it seven other spirits more wicked than itself, and they go in and live there. And the final condition of that person is worse than the first. That is how it will be with this wicked generation" (Matthew 12:43-45).

In the above verses, we see clearly many things about demons:

1) Demons can talk (verse 44): *"Then it says, 'I will return…'"*

2) Demon spirits can communicate with other demons (verse 45): *"Then it goes and takes with it seven other spirits more wicked than itself."*

3) Demons want a place to rest and they choose

human beings as their place to rest; they do not like to live in the wilderness or in a pit. *"When an unclean spirit goes out of a man, he goes through dry places, seeking rest."*

4) Demons call people their house. *"Then it (evils spirit) says, 'I will return to the house I left.'"*

The devil will always try to return after it has being cast out of a person. It will try to bring doubt into the person's heart (doubt about their deliverance), and/or it will try to manipulate the individual to make him say or do bad things so that it can return to his house.

The devil is very persistent in his attacks. Many times it will try to put the same sickness and disease right back after been healed. But fear not, because Jesus defeated them 2014 years ago on the cross for you and I. Amen!

Matthew 12: 45 states: "Then it goes and takes with it seven other spirits more wicked than itself, and they go in and live there. And the final condition of that person is worse than the first."

The devil's main purpose or mission in this life is to <u>steal</u>, to <u>kill</u>, and to <u>destroy</u> its victims. It is ONLY through Jesus Christ that you and I can have absolute victory over demons and all their hosts. Hallelujah!

CHAPTER 17

The Tenacity of Jesus Christ on Earth

◆

"Jesus said …follow me" (Mark 1:17)

As golden vessel we must clearly understand the tenacity of our Lord and savior Jesus Christ on earth. Why did He came? Why was He born of a virgin?

For this purpose the Son of God was manifested, that He might destroy the works of the devil (I John 3:8).

Jesus came into the world to destroy the works of satan. This immediately set Him in opposition to the enemy:

The thief cometh not, but for to steal, and to kill, and to destroy: I am come that they might have life and that they might have it more abundantly (John 10:10).

Follow Jesus!

Imitate and follow His footsteps. From the beginning

of His earthly ministry Jesus set about to destroy the works of satan:

- **Jesus Christ openly made known the bondage of sin** (John 8:34). He destroyed the works of satan in the hearts, souls, minds, and bodies of men and women: "The blind receive their sight, and the lame walk, the lepers are cleansed, and the deaf hear, the dead are raised up, and the poor have the Gospel preached to them" (Matthew 11:5). Jesus openly exposed the devious strategies of the devil so that we as Golden Vessels would not fall into the devil's schemes.

- **Jesus Christ taught on the deception of satan** which would increase during the last days on earth (Matthew 24-25).

- **The Son of man taught us of the necessity of binding the strong man (satan)** before he spoils the goods (Matthew 12:26-30; Mark 3:23-27; Luke 11:17-24).

- **Jesus openly revealed how satan tries to prevent the Word of God from being effective in the hearts of men.** He said: "The one who sowed the good seed is the Son of Man. The field is the world, and the good seed stands for the people of the kingdom. The weeds are the people of the evil one, and the enemy who sows them is the devil. The harvest is the end of the age, and the harvesters are angels" (Matthew 13:37-39).

- **He exposed those who were not right with God as being of their "father, the devil"** (John 8:44-47).

- **He revealed satan as the "prince of the world"** (John 14:30). "For this purpose the Son of God was manifested, that he might destroy the works of the devil" (1 John 3:8). Hatred, envy, jealousy, sickness, poverty, and spiritual death are all works of the devil. Jesus commands us, the believers, to destroy the works of the devil. Never lose sight of the fact that the devil has an unending desire to steal, kill, and destroy anything he can in your life.

- **Jesus called satan a "murderer"** (John 8:44).

- **You cannot sit with your hands folded and just watch the devil steal** your blessing, kill your potential, and destroy the lives of your loved ones. The devil is and will always be, 24 hours a day, 7 days a week "your **enemy**" (1 Peter 5:8). Heaven hates the devil with an everlasting hatred and so should you and I.

People of God, cloth yourself with the **full armor of God** [as Jesus Christ did] so that when the day of evil comes, you may be able to **stand your ground**, and after you have done everything, to stand. Stand firm then, with the belt of **truth** buckled around your waist, with the breastplate of **righteousness** in place, and with your feet fitted with the readiness that comes from the **gospel** of peace. Take up the shield of **faith**, with which you can extinguish all the flaming arrows of the evil one. Take the helmet of salvation and the sword of the **Spirit**, which is the **word** of God. And pray in the Holy

Spirit on all occasions with all kinds of prayers and requests (Ephesians 6:10-18).

Remember: the real enemy that we are fighting is the **devil** with all its hosts, including demon spirits, and dark angels. You are fighting a **spiritual** battle — **not your fellow human** beings. "For the weapons of our warfare are not carnal, but mighty through God to the pulling down of strong holds (2 Corinthians 10:4).

JESUS CHRIST IS THE PERFECT MODEL

Some of us choose the wrong person to be our role model. Sometimes the person we are imitating has behaviors and attitudes which are demonic, and many times while they are struggling with how to get rid of them, people on the other side want or desire to imitate them. The only perfect and sinless man who ever lived on earth is Jesus Christ. His life is without blemish. He knew no sin. "He bore our sins in his body on the cross, so that we might die to sins and live for righteousness; by his wounds you have been healed" (1 Peter 2:24-25).

Focus on the life of Christ and imitate Him entirely. Let it be your ultimate passion in life and ministry: be his imitator.

- Love the LORD your God with all your heart, with all your soul, with all your mind, and with all your strength.

- Love your neighbors as Jesus did.
- Heal the sick, cast out devils, and feed the needy as Jesus did.
- Be sensitive to hear and obey the voice of the Holy Spirit of God as Jesus did.

Follow the footsteps of Jesus Christ all the way. There is no one altogether lovely and powerful like Jesus! In spite of every man or woman of God in the Bible who God used at the golden level, there is none like Jesus. Let **Jesus Christ** be your **#1** perfect model in life. Hallelujah! Not Moses, not Peter, not Apostle Paul, not your father, nor your mother, not even your pastor or bishop, BUT Jesus Christ of Nazareth.

- Moses, whom the Bible says was more humble than any man on the face of the earth (Numbers 12:3), he was once so furious with his people that he struck a rock twice, something he was not supposed to do (Numbers 20:1–12). His temper got him in trouble.
- Peter, who was deeply zealous for Jesus, denied Him three times (Matthew 26:33–34).
- John, the beloved disciple who leaned on Jesus' bosom, was all ready to call down fire from heaven to destroy the inhabitants of Samaria who had rejected Jesus (Luke 9:52–54).
- Abraham, whom the Bible regards as a man of

faith (Hebrews 11:8–10), lied about his wife being his sister when a king coveted her. He endangered her life just to save his own skin (Genesis 20:1–18).

- What about Paul, the apostle of grace, who blazed the missionary trail which future missionaries would follow? Even the Apostle Paul went to Jerusalem when he was told not to by the Holy Spirit through the prophet Agabus (Acts 21:4, 10–11).

Saints, the best of us can fail. But there is ONE who cannot fail. His name is Jesus Christ. He is the only one who is faultless, flawless, sinless and altogether fitted to fulfill the work of God is Jesus Christ. And because He never misses the mark, you and I can look unto Him to be Golden Vessel in the hands of God for honorable service.

Look unto Jesus the author and finisher of our faith; who for the joy that was set before him endured the cross, despising the shame, and is set down at the right hand of the throne of God. Have faith in God.

CHAPTER 18

God Kind of Faith

♦

"And without faith it is impossible to please God, because anyone who comes to him must believe that he exists and that he rewards those who earnestly seek him." (Hebrews 11:6)

It requires faith to step into the golden vessel level. Faith is vital to be in the hands of God as golden vessel for honorable works. It requires faith to walk on water. It requires faith to please God. That faith will confuse your enemies. God kind of Faith demand for obedient to the voice of the Holy Spirit. The bible says, "Without faith it is impossible to please God".

WHAT IS GOD KIND OF FAITH?

Someone once said that faith is taking God seriously. It means to Say "YES to God and MOVE" in full obedience and reverence of what God said. Faith is the supernatural ability to believe God without doubt, unbelief, and visualize what God wants to accomplish. It is the supernatural ability to meet adverse circumstances, trials, red sea with trust in God words and messages. Faith is to trust God's Word without compromising or doubting of what the world or environment or anyone else have to say. In other words, God says it and you accept it without any objection. If God told you that you were beautiful, even if your face was like Shrek, you can only prosper when you believe and agree with the word you received from Him.

Hebrews 11:1 records that, "Faith is the reality of what is hoped for, the proof of what is not seen."

Faith is the substance of things hoped for, the evidence of things not seen. Faith requires that we follow the leading of the Holy Spirit. "For without faith it is impossible to please God." Many try so hard to please God with their head or their knowledge, but the Bible declares only faith pleases God, His kind of faith.

Faith demands trust in God. Proverbs 3:5 says, "Trust in the LORD with all your heart; do not depend on your own understanding." If you trust your own knowledge, you will miss the move of the God kind of faith I am talking about. "So faith comes from hearing, that is, hearing the Good News about Christ" (Romans 10:17).

To stand firm in these last days, saints, we need to have faith in God. We must trust and obey what God is saying to us in our particular situation. God designed that the 'just shall live by faith,' not by sight. Anyone can be changed by the God kind of faith, no matter how he may be fettered. I know that because God's Word is sufficient, it is eternal and it is trustworthy. One word from Him can change a nation for life. Have faith in the word of God. God's Word is from everlasting to everlasting.

"Man cannot live by bread alone but by every word that proceeds out of the mouth of God," said the begotten Son of God.

For centuries, people tried to discredit the Word of God and take from it all of the miraculous events which it records. One group says, "Well, you know, Jesus arranged beforehand to have that colt tied where it was, and for the men to say just what they did." I tell you, the Word of God is able to do the impossible. All things are possible to those who have faith or trust the word of the living God.

Other group says, "The Red Sea was only three feet deep so it was normal for the Israelites to walk in it." Just, because pharaoh's army drowned in a three feet water. That's a miracle.

Another group of critic says, "It was an easy thing for Jesus to feed the people with five loaves. The loaves were so big in those days that it was a simple matter to cut them into a thousand pieces each." But people with such thinking forgot that it was the lunch for a little boy. He brought those five loaves all the way in his lunch box. There is nothing impossible to those who believe, trust, and have faith in the Word of the Great I AM.

Faith is the confidence that what we hope for will actually happen; it gives us assurance about things we cannot see" (Hebrews 11:1). God kind of faith does crazy things. Noah built an ark on the top of a mountain, that's a crazy faith. Abraham offered his only son as a sacrifice unto God, that's a crazy faith. Peter walk on water, that's a crazy faith. To bring the good news of Jesus Christ around the world require God kind of faith

God kind of **Faith heals**. In my ministry, I have seen people healed from all kinds of sickness and diseases, like cancer, tumors, etc. I remember in a particular crusade in Haiti I prayed for a boy who was deaf. He was unable to hear for over ten years of his life, but after I prayed for him, instantly he was able to hear. Recently in a particular Revival in Oranger Jacmel Haiti, I prayed for a woman with an issue of blood for two years and she got healed instantly. Next day she came back testify the glory of God. I have seen people healed from terminal diseases within minutes. It is all because of faith in the Word of the Lord. The Word is powerful, sharper than any two edged sword. Glory to God!

In Mark 16:20, we read: "Then the disciples went out and preached everywhere, and the Lord worked with them and <u>confirmed</u> his word by the signs that accompanied it."

When you move with God kind of faith, the devil will tremble and flee from your presence. If you keep on walking in the God kind of faith surely you will come out with testimonies. Hallelujah!

TAKE THE LIMIT OFF

We must believe that nothing is too hard for God. It is a must for every Golden vessel to believe God for the impossible. God can do anything even the things that may seem impossible to human knowledge and understanding. God is omniscient. We ought to trust God to a point where nothing in this world troubles us. We must have confidence that He is able to show Himself strong on our behalf.

We cannot go higher than our thinking. We cannot be greater than what we think and believe we can. Jesus Christ taught that all things are possible to him that believes that it is possible.

Mark 9:23 Jesus said unto him, If thou canst believe, all things are possible to him that believeth.

This shows that man is always limited by his doubts and unbelief. If a man will not believe a thing is possible, it means he can't do it or attain it. If we will not believe we will be healed, it doesn't matter who prays for us, we won't be healed. If we do not believe that we will be promoted and continue to climb the ladder of success, we will remain on that same spot. If we do not believe that the business we are handling will be completed according to the original plan simply because there is a shortage of funds, it will be as we think. If we do not believe we can come out of lack and poverty, we will remain in that condition. If we do not believe we can be great though we came from a poor family and no one in our family has ever made it to the top or attained greatness, we will remain small, insignificant, poor, and a non-achiever. The truth of the matter is that every human is limited by his thinking and beliefs. That is why is it is important that we renewed our minds through the words of God and believe what it says and teaches. Every great man and woman you hear or read about it, had to take the limit off.

God's Golden vessels believe their needs can be met supernaturally. If human refused to obey to God, then Angel of God will do it. The angel fed Elijah in 1 Kings 19:5-6: "All at once an angel touched him and said, 'Get up and eat.' He looked around, and there by his head was some bread baked over hot coals, and a jar of water. He ate and drank and then lay down again."

They believe God for even water to come out of a rock as it happened to Moses. "'Strike the rock, and water will come out of it for the people to drink.' So Moses did this in the sight of the elders of Israel" (Exodus 17:6).

They believe that they can walk on water even though it is against the law of gravity. You only need to hear a word from God. Peter got down out of the boat, walked on the water and came toward Jesus (Mathew 14:29).

Recession is not a problem for a God's Golden Vessels; they believes money can come from even a fish's mouth. Jesus said: "Go to the lake and throw out your line. Take the first fish you catch; open its mouth and you will find a four-drachma coin. Take it and give it to them for my tax and yours."

They believe that prison doors can open without the help of human beings as it happened to Peter. "Suddenly, there was a massive earthquake, and the prison was shaken to its foundations. All the doors immediately flew open, and the chains of every prisoner fell off!" (Acts 16:26)**.**

They believe that they can get shelter without paying a penny. My wife and I once received a four bedroom house without any credit check, no money down, and no monthly mortgage payment. It was all by grace. Hallelujah!

God's golden vessels believe that people can be healed from any incurable genetic diseases. In my ministry, I have seen people healed from different kind of sicknesses. My sister prayed for a woman in a particular meeting who was diagnosed with three fibroid tumors and after we prayed for the woman she was instantly healed; miraculously when she consulted her doctor, the fibroids were all gone! The Lord dissolved those fibroid and tumors instantly, and the same year the woman gave birth to a healthy baby. Glory be to God! Hallelujah!

In May of 2013, I prophesied over a lady who was married for over seven years but never had any kids. Her doctors told her that it was impossible for her to carry a baby, because not only was she advanced in age, but her physical body was not well enough to carry a baby to term. The Spirit of the Lord told me to tell her that next year by this time she would have her own child in her hands and three months later she was pregnant. It was very difficult for her doctors to believe the pregnancy. They sent her to consult three different doctors to be sure! She was pregnant. "Glory to our God"! In June 21, 2014, she walked out of the hospital with her first child for the first time after eight years in marriage. God will do the impossible whenever we allow ourselves to be used as Golden Vessels.

Pray: *I pray that the Spirit of God will break every spirit of barrenness tormenting any area of your life in the name of Jesus. And if you desire a child, let the womb be opened in the name of Jesus!*

There is a level in God where your life becomes a life for the supernatural. It's called Golden Vessel. God is not an image, statue, or idol. He is real! Let Him be real in your life today and for the rest of your life. He is still the same yesterday, today, and forever.

CHAPTER 19
The Gifts and the Authority

♦

UNLOCKING DOORS

Golden vessels make a clear difference between the gifts vs the authority. There is a difference. The spiritual gifts help us to unlock spiritual doors and position us to be used more effectively in God's hands as vessels of honor. As Golden vessels, we must yield ourselves to the Holy Spirit, we need to desire to flow into the gifts of the Holy Spirit. The gifts open doors for us to see beyond the natural realm and they allow us to experience great manifestations of the power of God. Below are three categories of gifts we find in I Corinthians 12:

I. Vocal gifts are classified as prophecy, tongues, and interpretation of tongues.

II. Revelatory gifts are classified as word of knowledge, word of wisdom, and discerning spirits. It is something that you could not know by your natural mind; it is given by the Spirit of God.

III. Power gifts demonstrate the power of God. They are classified as faith, gifts of healing, and working of miracles.

The gifts work best for those who are thirsty and hunger for them. In the book of Isaiah, the Bible declares, is anyone thirsty? Come and drink—even if you have no money! Come, take your choice of wine or milk—it's all free! Again, in Isaiah 44 we read: "For I will pour water on him who is thirsty, And floods on the dry ground; I will pour My Spirit on your descendants, And My blessing on your offspring."

God will pour water upon those who are thirsty. It requires a deep thirst for the supernatural to be made manifest. It seems like no one is thirsty for the gifts of God. One thing about God's Golden Vessels is that they are not ashamed to ask of God and they are not ashamed to use or demonstrate them either. They ask Him so that they can be more effective or efficient in their God-given assignments.

"And so I tell you, keep on asking, and you will receive what you ask for. Keep on seeking, and you will find. Keep on knocking, and the door will be opened to you. For everyone who asks,

receives. Everyone who seeks, finds. And to everyone who knocks, the door will be opened" (Luke 11:9-11).

If you deny, doubt, and do not believe in the spiritual gifts, you will live a powerless and a defeated Christian life.

SUSPICIOUS IS NOT A GIFT FROM GOD

Suspicious or suspect is not a gift from God. Suspicious is built upon an accumulation of past hurts, past bitterness, past disagreements, and so forth. If we are going to look at people through the eyes of God Almighty, then we cannot carry a record of wrongs and suspect wrong of others. Jesus Christ was moved by compassion to forgive even His worst enemies; therefore, to operate effectively in the gifts of the Holy Spirit requires the indwelling of the love of God. "Love keeps no record of wrongs" (1 Corinthians 13:5). We are admonished to pursue love, and to desire spiritual gifts (1 Corinthians 14:1)

Jesus Christ gave gifts to the church (Ephesians 4:11-12).

Suspicious is from the pit of hell, it is NOT from the Lord. Now these are the gifts Christ gave to the church: the apostles, the prophets, the evangelists, the pastors, and teachers. Their responsibility is to perfecting God's people to do God's work and build up the church, the body of Christ.

These gifts are for the New Testament believers even some people say the contrary. Simply believe Christ and desire to receive His gifts, and you will see their manifestation in your life and ministry, because they are there for everyone who believes in Jesus, and those who are passionate about doing the work of the master, Jesus Christ.

I. Here is a list of the **gifts of the Holy Spirit for the Church**: (1 Corinthians 12; Romans 12)

- Word of wisdom   *Word of knowledge
- Faith   *Healings
- Working miracles *Prophecy
- Discerning of spirits
- Different kinds of tongues
- Interpretation of tongues.

II. **Here is a list of the fruit of the Holy Spirit** (Galatians 5:22-23): "love, joy, peace, longsuffering, gentleness, goodness, faith, meekness, temperance: against such there is no law." The fruits of the Holy Spirit must accompany the nine gifts of the Holy Spirit which we find in 1 Corinthians 12 or Romans 12 to be an effective minister of the Gospel.

If you live by the Holy Spirit, then walk in the Holy Spirit. The gifts are there to build up the body of

Christ, not for show business. The gifts edify the saints for the work of ministry and glorify God till we all come in the unity of the faith, and of the knowledge of the Son of God, unto a perfect man, unto the measure of the stature of the fullness of Christ. We as the church of Christ, need the gifts. Is there any evidence of the gifts in your life or in your local congregation? If so, great! Desire more and more, and if not, why settle for less?

Let us look at tongues, one of the gifts given to the church for personal edification:

Tongues For New Covenant Believers

Cease not to release mysteries through speaking in tongues. Jesus declared in Mark 16 that these signs will follow those who will believe: 'in my name they will speak with new tongues' (Mark 16: 17). He was not speaking about our native language, like English, Spanish, and so forth, or of someone who attended a traditional school to learn a new language. He was talking about the supernatural tongue from Heaven that the Holy Spirit, our Comforter, will enable us to speak. It is something that comes down from Heaven through the Holy Spirit.

We see evidence of people who supernaturally spoke in tongues instantly, and I am one of them.

Glory be to God. In Acts 2:3-4: "Then there appeared to them divided tongues, as of fire, and one sat upon each of them. And they were all filled with the Holy Spirit and began <u>to speak with other tongues</u>, as the Spirit gave them utterance."

In Acts 19:1-7, we see some believers who knew nothing about the gift of tongues. They gave an honest answer to the man of God and because of their readiness of hearts, they received the gift instantly through the laying on of hands.

In Acts 10, "While Peter was still speaking these words, the Holy Spirit fell upon all those who heard the word. And those of the circumcision who believed were astonished, as many as came with Peter, because the gift of the Holy Spirit had been poured out on the Gentiles also. For they heard them speak with tongues and magnify God."

I received my heavenly language in the middle of the night around 4:00 – 5:00 am. I woke up and I found myself praying in tongues; I could not say anything in English or Creole. I heard myself saying some wonderful things like someone who speaks the Hebrew language. From that day forward, I spoke in tongues and my life has been changed. I cannot spend a day without reading my Bible and prayer! After that experience I become more in love with God and I had a deeper and a stronger desire to know Jesus more and more.

I have met with people who knew nothing about

the gift of tongues or who were skeptical about it, yet they acted as though they knew it all; they would not listen but simply made blanket statements. One pastor told me that this praying in tongues business is nonsense; one told me that you learn tongues when you go to school; another told me the gift of tongues is inferior. Did Jesus lied to us? When He said in Mark 16:17-18 in my name they shall speak new tongues? In Acts 19, we saw those believers who believed in the word that Paul preached to them and they received the gift! In our meetings, we have seen hundreds of people receive the gift of tongues. They were able to pray as you will see in the verses below:

> **And it happened, while Apollos was at Corinth, that Paul, having passed through the upper regions, came to Ephesus. And finding some disciples he said to them, "Did you receive the Holy Spirit when you believed?" So they said to him, "We have not so much as heard whether there is a Holy Spirit."**

> **And when <u>Paul had laid hands on them</u>, the Holy Spirit came upon them, and <u>they spoke with tongues and prophesied</u>. Now the men were about twelve in all.**

Some may argue that this tongues the Bible is referring to was only for the disciples in the first century church; but nowhere in the Bible does it state that "speaking in tongues" is not for us today. Speaking in tongues are for every born again believer. If you believe, you shall see; and if you ask, you shall receive.

"For he who speaks in a tongue does not speak to men but to God, for no one understands him; however, in the spirit he speaks mysteries" (1 Corinthians 14:2). Beloved, if you desire to speak to God, and Him alone, then pray in tongues. You can spend hours non-stop talking to Him! While you are doing that, remember you are speaking mysteries and edifying yourself and glorifying God.   Hallelujah!

Jude 20 states, "But you, beloved, building yourselves up on your most holy faith, praying in the Holy Spirit."

Beloved, cease not to pray in tongues, even when no one else understands you. They should not anyway because the Bible clearly says: "For he who speaks in a tongue does <u>*not speak to men but to God*</u>, for no one understands him; however, in the spirit he speaks mysteries" (1 Corinthians 14:2).

SUBMIT TO AUTHORITY

One thing I see that causes so much division in the body of Christ is the misconception of the gift vs the authority. Having the gift is one thing, being established in the office is another. In 1 Corinthians 12:7, it states: "A spiritual gift is given to each of us so we can help each other. To one person the Spirit gives the ability to give wise advice."

You can minister powerfully under a special gift and yet not be established in the authority of that office. King Saul prophesied under the gift of prophecy, but Samuel was established in the office of a prophet.

You receive authority when you are established in a particular office of ministry. For example, Miriam operated with the gift; she was a prophetess. But Moses was established in the office of Prophet; Moses received authority from God for that office of ministry.

In a local church, many people may have different gifts, but there is someone whom God places in authority and the rest of the people must acknowledge that person. In other words, there is someone who carry the vision and he/she deserves to be acknowledged and shown great respect.

Korah and his friends were ministers in the gifts, not in authority; they incited rebellion against Moses their leader, the one whom God gave the vision to, and as a result they died.

"They united against Moses and Aaron and said, …What right do you have to act as though you are greater than the rest of the LORD's people?'" (Number 16:3). Notice, they began to minimize Moses' authority by saying: "What right do you have to act as though you are greater than the rest of the LORD's people?" It does not matter how powerful you are when you minister under the gift, you still need to listen to authority. If the pastor of that congregation says, "Do this or do that," and you say, "Yes," and then you fail to do it, you are disobeying him.

If you are speeding and a police officer stops you, you need to listen and obey what they tell you to do (as long as they do not tell you to oppose the Word of God) for they have been placed in authority. Many traffic violators get arrested or charged a huge fine because they refuse to do the very simple thing that the police officer ask them to do.

Jesus is the perfect example on how to submit to authority. He submitted Himself totally to God the Father even unto His death on the cross.

"Who, being in the form of God, thought it not robbery to be equal with God: But made himself of no reputation, and took upon him the form of a servant, and was made in the likeness of men: And being found in fashion as a man, he humbled himself, and became obedient unto death, even the death of the cross. Wherefore God also hath highly exalted him, and given him a name which is above every name: That at the name of Jesus every knee should bow, of things in heaven, and things in earth, and things under the earth; And that every tongue should confess that Jesus Christ is Lord, to the glory of God the Father" (Philippians 2:6-11).

Jesus entered a human courtroom, and did not say anything. He did not curse or say any filthy words to those who had put Him on trial. The chief priest, the governor, and high priest tore His clothes and slapped Him, but He did not say one word.

Submit yourself to the divine order of God:

- Jesus submitted Himself to God.
- Men and women must submit themselves to Jesus Christ.
- A wife must submit herself to her husband in the Lord.
- Children must submit to their parents in the Lord.

Be submissive to authority in the Lord for it is good. Amen.

EMBRACING GRATITUDE

"In everything give thanks; for this is God's will for you in Christ Jesus" (I Thessalonians 5:18).

As you submit to authority and minister into the gifts embracing gratitude. It is the perfect will of God for us to live a life of gratitude. Most of us are living a life of ingratitude, why? Because we are not giving thanks to God in the way we ought to. We are not showing gratitude to God the way we supposed to do it. God deserve more and more, reverence, honor, adoration, and so on in a level that exceed our routine way of doing thing.

Romans 1:21 says, "Yes, they knew God, but they wouldn't worship Him as God or even give Him thanks. And they began to think up foolish ideas of what God was like. As a result, their minds became dark and confused."

They know Him, but they don't glorify Him as God, nor give Him thanks as God, their heart is not in what they do. God wants us to show our gratitude even in the midst of our storms and the darkest moments of life. In everything, give Him thanks for it is the perfect will of God for us. Always give thanks. It is time to show gratitude to God for what He has done in your life. Give Him thanks for every single part of your body. Take some quality time to give Him thanks for the visible as well as the invisible things in your life and family. Give Him thanks for putting your name in the Book of Life (if you are born again). Give Him thanks for the blood of Jesus, the birds that sing, the oxygen, the ants that teach wisdom, the cow that gives milk; the list goes on. Give Him thanks for the Holy Spirit as your comforter, guide, and teacher. Give Him thanks!

Psalms 103 states Bless the Lord, O my soul: and all that is within me, bless his holy name. Bless the Lord, O my soul, and forget not all his benefits: Who forgiveth all thine iniquities; who healeth all thy diseases; Who redeemeth thy life from destruction; who crowneth thee with lovingkindness and tender mercies; Who satisfieth thy mouth with good things; so that thy youth is renewed like the eagle's.

Ungrateful people only complain about their present state or situation. They grumble for things that are perishing like food, money, houses, cars, etc. They easily forget all the good things that have happened, and all that God has done for them. My advice to you is to flee from ungrateful folks, and if you are one, repent! God wants us to show gratitude unto Him as well as to others.

UNGRATEFULNESS IS SIN.

"And when the people complained, it displeased the LORD: and the LORD heard it; and his anger was kindled; Who shall give us flesh to eat? They asked. We remember the fish, which we did eat in Egypt freely; the cucumbers, and the melons, and the leeks, and the onions, and the garlic" (Numbers 4:1-5).

The ungrateful people stressed out and died in the wilderness. Many Israelites (about fourteen thousands and seven hundred in total), died in one day because they were complaining and murmuring for food. This type of behavior and attitude gave satan ground in their lives. It attracted a curse.

Now, let's look at the ungrateful lepers. Jesus healed ten lepers, but only one came back to give thanks.

And as he entered into a certain village, there met him ten men that were lepers, which stood afar off: And they lifted up their voices, and said, "Jesus, Master, have mercy on us."

And when he saw them, he said unto them, "Go shew yourselves unto the priests." And it came to pass, that, as they went, they were cleansed. And one of them, when he saw that he was healed, turned back, and with a loud voice glorified God, And fell down on his face at his feet, giving him thanks: and he was a Samaritan.

And Jesus answering said, "Were there not ten cleansed? but where are the nine? There are not found that returned to give glory to God, save this stranger" (Luke 17:13-18).

An ungrateful attitude will stop your next miracle, but a grateful heart attracts the blessings of God. "Give thanks in all circumstances, for this is God's will for you in Christ Jesus" (1 Thessalonians 5:18).

Psalm 136 says, "Oh, give thanks to the LORD, for He is good!(For His mercy endures forever. (Oh, give thanks to the God of gods!(For His mercy endures forever. (Oh, give thanks to the Lord of lords! For His mercy endures forever…

Golden vessels praise and give thanks to God in everything—for what He did for them yesterday, last week, last month, and so forth. And the good news is, while they are magnifying God above and beyond their present circumstances, God in return moves on their behalf and makes a way for them in the present. They simply trust and believe the Word of God that says: "I will never leave you nor forsake you."

No matter what comes your way, know that God will be with you and He will guide and instruct you. Gratefulness toward Him and toward other people around you will provoke your life to rise and shine.

CHAPTER 20

It's Time to Arise & Shine

◆

Isaiah 60:1 says, "Arise, shine, for your light has come, and the glory of the LORD rises upon you."

It is time for every golden vessel to arise and shine. Do not be afraid to step up and shine for God. Please note that you cannot shine unless you first arise. God is calling us to step up and shine for His glory. Your family must rise and shine. Your children must rise and shine. Your business must rise and shine. Your ministry must arise and shine. We are the light of the world, therefore, it is vital for the light to shine. Do not be partakers with darkness; for you were formerly darkness, but now you are light in the Lord; walk as children of light (for the fruit of the light consists in all goodness and righteousness and truth), trying to learn what is pleasing to the Lord. And do not participate in the unfruitful deeds of darkness, but instead even expose them; for it is disgraceful even to speak of the things which are done by them in secret. But all things become visible when they are exposed by the light, for everything that becomes visible is light.

For this reason it says, "Awake, sleeper, And arise from the dead, And Christ will shine on you."

Saints, it is time for us to arise and take our authority and our position in Christ and let that light shine on this dark world. This is the plan of God, and He definitely plans to work through you, His Golden Vessels. He is looking for a vessel that He can use as a point of contact to spark revival.

If you're still complaining and murmuring, then you have not yet risen and you are not yet shining. If you still doubt God or the Word of the Lord, then you have not yet risen and you are not yet shining.

Matthew 5:14-16 declares: "You are the light of the world. A city that is set on a hill cannot be hidden. Nor do they light a lamp and put it under a basket, but on a lampstand, and it gives light to all who are in the house. Let your light so shine before men, that they may see your good works and glorify your Father in heaven."

In a world full of darkness, sin, perversion, stress, crime, and hatred, God needs people who will stand like Shadrach, Meshach, and Abed-Nego to shine for

Jesus. These boys knew their God, and refused to walk in darkness. In the midst of a dark hour, when people stand against you and say all kind of evil things against you, can you still shine like a bright light?

The answer is "Yes" you can, because you received the Holy Spirit. God gave us the ability to walk in the path of Jesus. God gave you all the benefits and privileges that Jesus has. The Bible declares that we have the mind of Christ (I Corinthians 2:16). We share one spirit with the Lord…But whoever is united with the Lord is one with him in spirit (1 Corinthians 6:17).

Arise and shine! There are things in your life that will not happen until you arise. The lady with the issue of blood would not have received her healing until she arose and went to touch Jesus' garment. Demons will not flee until you and I arise and go ahead and cast them out in the name of Jesus.

Lack of knowledge will not leave us until you and I arise and seek to know God in an intimate way day after day and night after night. God told Joshua, "This book of the law shall not depart out of thy mouth; but thou shalt meditate therein day and night, that thou mayest observe to do according to all that is written therein: for then thou shalt make thy way prosperous, and then thou shalt have good success." He told Joshua what to do if Joshua wanted to be prosperous and have good success in life. That's it. Today, He tells us to step up and shine!

Brethren, either we believe the Word of God, or we don't. The word in our mouth will turn night into day. You shall decree a thing, and it shall be established for you; and the light [of God's favor] shall shine upon your ways. Your life will illuminate when you speak the Word of God every day. For the Word is a lamp unto our feet, it is turned on when the Word of God is released from our mouth daily.

If you arise and shine as light in the world, that light will illuminate your world. Remember the devil can only exist in darkness. Step up! Rise up and shine.

Pray this prayer: (1) I will arise and shine. (2) I will rise up and shine to glorify the King of glory for I am not in this world in vain. In Jesus' Name. I shall walk in obedience and reverence of my LORD in Jesus name. My life is hidden in Christ Jesus! Amen!

CHAPTER 21

Shema and Yirah God

◆

> "...Obedience is better than sacrifice, and submission is better than offering the fat of rams [1 Samuel 15:22b].

The secret of every Golden Vessel is shema and Yirah unto God. ["Shema means obeying, listening, taking heed, and responding with action to what one has heard from God". Yirah means reverence and awe to God. Obedience and reverence are the ultimate secrets to everyone who wants to be a Golden Vessel in the hands of God. If you miss everything else I have said in this book, don't miss this: seek shema and yirah unto God.

> "In a great house there are not only vessels of gold and of silver, but also of wood and of clay; and some to honour, and some to dishonour. If a man therefore purge himself from these, he shall be a vessel unto honour, sanctified, and meet for the master's use, and prepared unto every good work" (2 Timothy 2:20-21).

In the church, there valued prized clean and beautify utensils that are used to serve the food. But there also cheap, ugly, plastic plates. Some people are prized, valued to serve the Lord, as noble, useful, having been sanctified, having been prepared. Others are disgraceful, should never appear in public at all. It is talking about the double minded, the deceivers, the false brothers and the yeast of the Pharisees and everyone else who is practicing, and living in wickedness right in the house of God. If you desire to be use as golden vessel, you must flee from them. Flee from youthful lust and sexual immorality and seek to obey your Heavenly Father. We must cleanse ourselves from these, then we will be vessels for honor, sanctified, useful to the master, prepared for every good work. Learn to pour out your heart to God and for Him in everything. Reverence Him.

Psalms 16:8 states: "I have set the LORD always before me; because he is at my right hand, I shall not be shaken." David obedience pushed him to place God before everything else.

Reverence and obedience are the ultimate keys to use in other to get to that level of vessels of honor. I am **NOT** talking about terror, or dread, such as:

- Fear of man (gangsters, murders, thefts, etc.)
- Fear of the economy (worry of losing a car, a home, jobs, etc.)

- Fear of demon spirits (afraid to go to sleep, etc.

But I am talking about honoring God, the willingness to do what He asked you to do, where you esteem Him above everything else in your life. I am talking about trusting the Lord, having a deeper respect for Him, revere Him, loving Him, and honoring Him.

OBEDIENT UNTO GOD OPEN UP UNLOCKING DOOR…

God told Abraham to give his only son Isaac. He did not doubt the voice of God. He said, 'Ok, Lord, I'll be obedient to you.'

The Holy Spirit told Philip, "Go to that chariot and stay near it." Then Philip ran up to the chariot (Acts 8:29-30 NIV). He trusted and obeyed the voice of the Holy Spirit because of his deep reverence for God.

How can we comprehend the utterly Great News of Jesus Christ if we don't first understand the yirah [reverence] and the shema [obedience] of God? Jesus Christ Himself delighted in the obedience of God His father. He did what He saw His father doing. He reverenced His father to a point where He did whatever the Father asked Him to do—even to the point of dying for mankind.

He said: "Very truly, I tell you, the Son can do nothing by himself; he can do only what He sees His Father doing, because whatever the Father does the Son also does. For the Father loves the Son and shows Him all He does. Yes, and He will show him even greater works than these, so that you will be amazed (John 5:19-20 NIV).

God look on those who reverence Him, and He moves mightily on their behalf. Second Chronicles 16:9 says, "For the eyes of the LORD run to and fro throughout the whole earth, to shew himself strong in the behalf of them whose heart is perfect toward him. Herein thou hast done foolishly."

"He provides food for those who reverence him; He remembers His covenant forever" (Psalm 111:5). Obey the Lord so that you may prosper and be kept alive. Obedience **to God keeps us from sinning** (Exodus 20:20). Obey the Lord and serve Him with all faithfulness. Throw away the gods your forefathers worshiped beyond the River and in Egypt, and serve the Lord.

"The eyes of the Lord are on those who yirah Him, on those whose hope is in His unfailing love, to deliver them from death and keep them alive in famine" (Psalm 33:18-19).

Deliverance of the Lord is near those who yirah God (Psalm 85:9).

"God takes pleasure in those who Yirah Him (those who have reverence for Him); He fulfills the desires of those who obey Him; he hears their cry and saves them.

He watches over all who love him" (Psalm 145:19-20; Psalm 147:11).

Our obedience to God prove our love for Him (1 John 5:2-3), it demonstrates our faithfulness to Him (1 John 2:3-6), glorifies Him in the world (1 Peter 2:12), and opens avenues of blessing for us (John 13:17).

The midwives were obedient to God to a point that they disobeyed the wicked command of pharaoh, placing their lives in great danger; but it is better to obey God, rather than man. "they feared God, and did not as the king of Egypt commanded them, but saved the men children alive" (Exodus 1:17).

Angels are obedient to God. They are ready to go wherever God sends them and do whatever He asks them to do. That qualifies them to be Golden Vessels in the hands of God. They know that God is not a man to lie or a son of man not able to carry out His promises, so they obey God regardless of the cost.

Psalm 103:20 says, "Praise the Lord, you his angels, you mighty ones who do his bidding, who obey his word."

We serve a holy God; therefore, we must walk in obedience, reverence and holiness, as all His holy angels do. If He says we can, then we can walk in holiness.

CHAPTER 22

In Closing...

♦

"In a great house there are not only vessels of gold and of silver, but also of wood and of clay; and some to honour, and some to dishonor" (2 Timothy 2:20).

God is looking for Golden Vessels to use for honorable works of ministry and one of those vessels can be you. Are you one of them? He does not look at your past to determine your future. God does not focus on your past failure, your educational background, your height, or even your position in the society. If you can step out from your comfort zone, and say, "Lord, here I am. I abandon myself to You. Use me! Mold me! And Purge me," then you will be amazed what God can and will do with you.

My prayer for you is that the Lord will take the things I've shared and bring you into a new understanding of the characteristics of God's Golden Vessels, and also that you will yield yourself to be one with God so that God can use you whenever and however He pleases. It does not come automatically; it takes discipline. But by seeking the Lord with your whole heart, dwelling in His Word, and staying obedient to the Holy Spirit, praying and fasting, then you will definitely reach that level of gold God desired you to be.

Surely Jesus Will Not Put Away Anyone Who Comes To Him With A Sincere Heart. John 6:37 says, "All whom My Father gives (entrusts) to Me will come to Me; and the one who comes to Me I will most certainly not cast out [I will never, no never, reject one of them who comes to Me]" (AMP).

God knows your name and your address, and when you answer His call, He will change you into the very image of His Son, Jesus Christ, and move you from clay to gold. He did it for Jacob, Moses, Apostle Paul and many more.

Genesis 27 record that God called Jacob while he was a deceiver.

Jacob who was once a deceiver is now called Israel. God is still looking for people to use as Golden Vessels. Society, family, and friends may have rejected you, but God is still waiting on you to answer His call to make you a Golden Vessel.

Genesis 32:28 reads: "And He said, Your name shall be called no more Jacob [supplanter], but **Israel** [contender with God]; for you have contended and have power with God and with men and have prevailed." God changed his name and his destiny. He can do it for you if you sincere about serving Him.

God called Saul of Tarsus while he was a criminal, and a murderer of the saints.

In Acts 9:1-6 we read: Meanwhile Saul, still drawing his breath hard from threatening and murderous desire against the disciples of the Lord, went to the high priest. And requested of him letters to the synagogues at Damascus [authorizing him], so that if he found any men or women belonging to the Way [of life as determined by faith in Jesus Christ], he might bring them bound [with chains] to Jerusalem. And he fell to the ground. Then he heard a voice saying to him, Saul, Saul, why are you persecuting Me [harassing, troubling, and molesting Me]?

And Saul said, Who are You, Lord? And He said, I am Jesus, Whom you are persecuting. It is dangerous and it will turn out badly for you to keep kicking against the goad [to offer vain and perilous resistance].

God called Moses while he was a murderer.

Exodus 2:12 says, "He looked this way and that way, and when he saw no one, he killed the Egyptian and hid him in the sand."

When God calls someone, He has a purpose for

him—to change that person into the image of His Son, Jesus Christ. He does not focus on your past failure. Instead, the question is, are you be willing to be that vessel of honor He wants you to become? Have a deep passion to please God above all things. Believe and delight yourself in Him and you will see His glory overshadow your life. If God can use me, the Apostle Paul (Saul), the Apostle Peter, and many more, He can use you also. God is the same yesterday, today, and forever (Hebrews 13:8).

Today Choose For Yourself

Either we sincerely serve God and become all that He wanted us to be, or serve Baal; but **NOT** both. And if we choose to serve God, don't fake it! Serve Him with our whole heart. Let's be bold as a lion. God's Golden Vessels do not care of what man might say about them; they chose Christ and they chose Him fully. They have no fear of what man might say because they know that obedient is better than sacrifice. Let's arise and be part of the company of God's Golden Vessels and nothing less. Amen! Amen.

If You're Not BORN AGAIN, You're Not Safe! Receive Jesus Christ into your Heart Today!

◆

WELCOME JESUS CHRIST INTO YOUR HEART TODAY

If Jesus Christ calls you today, do you know where you stand with God?

If you have never made Jesus Christ the Lord of your life, then you are estranged from God by sin. You are the very reason God sent Jesus to the cross. John 3:16 says, "For God *loved* the world so much that he gave his one and only Son, Jesus Christ, so that everyone who believes in him will not perish but have eternal life" (NLT). God *loved you* so much that He gave His only begotten Son for you.

Second Corinthians 5:21 says that God made Jesus, who knew no sin, to be sin for us. Sin was the reason Jesus came to earth. He died on the cross and went to hell for one reason: to pay the price for sin. Once that price was paid, Jesus was raised from the dead, triumphant over Satan. The sin problem was taken care of. God does not hold your sin against you. You have the right to choose your own destiny; God will not force you to receive salvation. You can go straight to hell and God will not lift a finger to stop you. He did all He is going to do when He sent Jesus Christ into the world.

If you do choose to make Jesus your Lord, God will receive you as His very own child.

Enter the Prayer Room

EXPECT HEALING AND DELIVERANCE AS YOU BOLDLY CONFESS THESE PRAYER POINTS.

◆

PRAYER FOR HEALING TO YOUR BODY

If you have any pain, sickness or diseases to your body believe God, now as you confess these prayers for your total healing and deliverance in Jesus name:

1 Peter 2:24 says, "Who his own self bore our sins in His own body on the tree that we, being dead to sins, should live unto righteousness: by whose stripes ye were healed."

Psalm 103:1-3 says, "Bless the Lord O my soul, and all that is within me, bless His Holy name. Bless the Lord O my soul and forget not all His benefits. Who forgiveth all thine iniquities, who healeth all thy diseases."

Now Pray:

Father God, Your scripture says that you heal all diseases and whoever believes in Your Son Jesus will not perish but have an everlasting life. Strengthen me, Father, in this time of illness. When You were on Earth, you did all things good and healed all kinds of sickness.

You healed those who had diseases. You died and rose for our sins and that we may have eternal life, Lord. I believe in my heart that You are here with us today and that with Your most holy power will remove all sicknesses and evils that roam the earth.

1. By the power in the shed blood of Jesus Christ, I declare that I am healed from the top of my head to the sole of my feet in Jesus Name.

2. My body is the temple of the Holy Spirit, therefore any pain, sickness and diseases in my body you are illegal, leave me now in the name of Jesus.

3. Every germ of sickness and diseases anywhere in my body I command and charge you to die right now, in the name of Jesus.

4. **Point your finger to any part of your body where you feel any pain and say:** You demon of sickness leave my body right now in the name of Jesus. Leave my body in Jesus Name [repeat 12 times].

5. I am free! I am free and free in the mighty name of Jesus. Amen.

NOW DO WHAT YOU COULD NOT DO BEFORE!!!

Write me to let me know how Jesus Christ healed you!!

RISE UP IN CHRIST JESUS…

- Forgive and love others as the Lord Himself forgave and loves you.
- Praise God and give Him thanks for who He is in your life.

Now pray these prayer points with faith and boldness in God:

1. I cover myself with the precious blood of Jesus. Let the power in the blood of Jesus separate me from the sins of my ancestors. I am a child of the living God! My name is written in the book of life. I boldly declare and decree that I am not in this world in vain, in the mighty name of Jesus.

2. Father God, let the anointing of the Holy Spirit break every yoke of backwardness and failure in my life, my family and ministry, in the name of Jesus. Let my life be saturated with the powerful blood of Jesus Christ of Nazareth.

3. I command every spiritual contamination in my life, in my calling to receive cleansing by the blood of Jesus Christ. I use the blood of Jesus to wash away all dirtiness in my spirit, soul, and body, in the name of Jesus.

4. I command every power eating up my spiritual life to be roasted, and become powerless, and I renounce any evil dedication placed upon my life and my position in God, in the unquenchable name of Jesus.

5. I renounce and loose myself from every negative influence placed upon my life, my calling, and my gifts, and I unplug and disconnect myself from every evil inherited covenant, and I connect myself fully to the Holy Ghost, the power source of life, in the Mighty name of Jesus.

6. I cancel the consequences of all and any evil local names attached to my person, my family and my ministry and I bind and drive out all principalities and powers operating over and within my heart and my calling, in the name of Jesus. I am anointed with the Holy Spirit and power. So I cast out any wrong presence in my environment, in the name of Jesus.

7. I am a winner, a successful child, and a triumphant being for life through the blood of Jesus, and I bind and cast out every evil power pulling anything in my soul and body, in the name of Jesus.

8. I command every evil tree, evil altars, and plantation against my calling to receive Holy Ghost fire and be destroy to their roots, in the glorious name of Jesus.

9. Every spirit of confusion and evil mind control assigned against my life, my calling and my ministry loose your hold, in the name of Jesus. And anything from the kingdom of darkness that has made it their business to frustrate my calling, receive an angelic slap and Holy Ghost fire, in the name of Jesus.

10. I reject every demonic limitation and backwardness on my progress, in the name of Jesus. I declare that I am called of God; no evil power shall cut me down, in the name of Jesus. Father God, help me to be faithful to my calling, in the name of Jesus.

11. I receive power, authority, and dominion to rise up and shine, with wings as eagles everywhere I go. The devil will not eat up my ministerial destiny, and I shall not be an enemy of integrity and holiness, in the glorious name of Jesus.

12. I shall not disgrace the call of God upon my life, in the name of Jesus. I shall work in holiness every day of my life and be that Golden Vessel God has called me to be, in the glorious name of Jesus.

13. I am standing on the good ground of the Word of God to be that vessel of honor God called me to be and no power of hell can remove me, and I sign these declarations with Holy Ghost fire, and the blood of Jesus in the mighty name of Jesus. Amen! Amen! Amen!

BREAK THE WEAPONS OF YOUR ENEMIES -- PRAYER POINTS

1. Holy Spirit push me where God originally planned for me to be, in the mighty name of Jesus Christ! (2 times)

2. I refuse to die in the wilderness of life. Every voice speaking against my destiny, shut up forever in

the mighty name of Jesus (2 times)

3. I shall not die without accomplishing my divine purpose in life, in the awesome name of Jesus! I reject every form of witchcraft against my life, in the name of Jesus.

4. No weapons fashioned against my destiny will prosper and every evil tongue prophesying against my vision shall be made null and void, in the name of Jesus (2 times).

5. I shall arise and shine, in the name of Jesus! My finances shall rise! My children shall rise! My family shall rise! My destiny shall rise and shine, in the mighty name of Jesus.

6. Today, I cancel and bring to naught every unprofitable project, plan, and gathering against my destiny. I refuse to use my tongue or any part of my body to speak against my divine destiny, in the name of Jesus (3 times).

7. I reject and nullify every satanic alternative for my destiny, in the mighty name of Jesus. I clothe myself with the garment of fire, in the precious name of Jesus. Amen!

8. My destiny is hidden in Christ Jesus and every destiny swallower, I force you out of my way, in the name of Jesus.

9. Every gathering of darkness against my destiny anywhere in the world, scatter like dust, in the name of

Jesus. And I refuse to miss my divine destiny in life, in the name of Jesus. My destiny will be established whether the devil likes it or not, in the name of Jesus. It is done. Amen! Amen! Amen!

I AM IN CHRIST – PRAYER POINTS

If you are serious about becoming a golden vessel in the hand of God confess this prayer at least twice per day for at least 7 days:

- I am a spirit, I have a soul, and I live in a body, but I am first a spirit being – BORN OF GOD.
- I am in Christ and He is made unto me wisdom, righteousness, sanctification, and redemption. Therefore, I am righteous in Christ Jesus and I have His wisdom. I am sanctified and redeemed by His blood.
- I have a nature of faith, because faith works by love, and the love of God has been SHED ABROAD in my heart by the Holy Ghost, who has been given to me. [Romans 5:5]
- I am born of God. I am OF God. I am a spirit being – born of God. I am justified by FAITH; therefore I have peace with God.
- I am a new creature in Christ, the old things have

passed away, behold all things have become new. I have a new nature. It's the nature of God. It's the nature of love, for love is of God. [1 John 4:7]

- I have been given the privilege of becoming a child of God. I am God's very own child and God is my very own Father. [John 1:12 & Romans 8:15]

- Because I am His child, I am an heir of God and a joint heir with Jesus Christ. [Romans 8:17]

- I have faith in God. I believe in Christ, and I am in Him. I believe He is able and faithful to do the impossible in my life in Jesus Name.

- I have received abundance of grace and the gift of righteousness and I reign in this life through Jesus Christ. [Rom 5:17] I receive and reign through Jesus Christ.

- I have been delivered from the power and dominion of darkness (Satan) and I have been translated into the kingdom of God's dear Son.

- I am presented to God holy, blameless, and irreproachable in His sight, and right now I am freely accepted by Him through His grace in the name of Jesus

- As a Believer, in the Name of Jesus Christ, I cast out devils, I speak with new tongues, and I lay hands on the sick and they do recover. (Mark

16:17-18)

- I am what the word of God says that I am. I am the head and will never be the tail; I am above and I refuse to be beneath in the mighty name of Jesus. This year all my enemies will see me flourishing like trees planting by the stream of water.
- This year I shall dance with overwhelm Joy, peace and love and I shall dance in triumph and victory over my present situation in the mighty name of Jesus.
- I am blessed with all spiritual blessings in heavenly places in Christ, and I stand holy and without blame before Him in love. Hallelujah!

If you are one of God's golden Vessels, Make **12** Shout of **"Hallelujah"** after today my life, my ministry and my family will never be the same again. I am a golden Vessel, washed, sanctified through the blood of Jesus and to please my God all the day of my life. Amen.

A LETTER TO MY HEAVENLY FATHER:

Holy Father,

I join my heart and my voice with all the holy angels,

and the saints of God to declare and decree, "Holy, holy, holy is the Lord God Almighty, who was and is, and is to come." Jesus Christ is worthy, my Lord and my God, to receive glory and honor and power, for He created all things and by His will they were created and have their being (Revelation 4:8, 11).

Thank Father for your Son Jesus Christ who died on the cross and made it possible for all of us to become vessel of Honor, sanctified, holy and acceptable to God to His will on here on Earth.

Please come, Jesus! And may the grace of the Lord Jesus Christ be with all God's people. Amen!

From your son,

Yves P. Beauvais, a servant of the Lord

THE MYSTERY OF GOD'S GOLDEN VESSELS

This book contains revelations which will stir up your spirit to move you from the valley of stagnancy to the mountain top of mighty men and women of honor. There is something exceptional and explosive when God's Golden Vessels practice obedience and show forth a willingness to dwell at the feet of God and ready to carry out his honorable assignments. This book will challenge you to join the company of sons and daughters of God who are connected to the source of unlimited signs, wonders, and miracles through uncommon commitment and obedience. It is powerfully presented and illustrated in an easy way. The Mystery of God's Golden Vessels is a guide to countless positions of honor right in the hand of Almighty God. Every child of God is called to be a Golden Vessel. Hallelujah!

Pastor Yves helps readers unveil the mystery of Golden Vessels in the hands of God. Few of us barely get to the edge of that level of honor. Before Jesus returns, I prophesy, there is going to be a whole company of Christian believers—children, youth, and adults, me and women—who will rise from their comfort zones and become the Golden Vessels that God wants them to be. They will be pure as gold and will do the works of the Kingdom with unusual signs, wonders, and creative miracles by the power of the Holy Ghost in the Name of Jesus Christ of Nazareth. Amen!

"In a great house there are not only vessels of GOLD and of SILVER, but also of WOOD and OF CLAY; and some to honour, and some to dishonor" (2 Timothy 2:20).

Friend, be golden vessel in the Hands of God today and nothing less in Jesus Name. Amen. Amen.

About the Author

Pastor Yves' birth was a miracle. His mother carried him in her womb for over two years, in a small town in Haiti. She went to different clinics and consulted many native doctors for help, but they could not do anything to help her. But when God roars all his enemies scattered. He rose up with His mighty hands and removed all form of darkness that was preventing Pastor Yves from coming into this world. Miraculously, his mother gave birth to him. And now his is preaching the gospel of Jesus. Hallelujah!

The ministry of Pastor Yves reaches thousands of people through radio broadcasting, teleconference, Bible teaching, and preaching. His strong pastoral thrust displays the strength of the mandate upon his life. He hosts miracle and healing revivals throughout the country, including but not limited to the U.S., Canada, Haiti, etc. The uplifting message Pastor Yves brings has ministered grace, healing, and has transformed lives all over the world. He is a flaming minister with a divine purpose to destroy the works of darkness and build the Kingdom of God.

Pastor Yves resides in Florida with his wife, Joy Rose, and their three children: Jemimah, Yochanan Akim, and Prince Joash Beauvais.

References

Unless otherwise identified, Scripture quotations are from New King James Version of the Bible

Immanuel, Stella "ATTACKING THE ENEMY OF YOUR CALLING." N.p., n.d. Web. 24 Oct. 2014

Jordan, E. Bernard "Praise and Worship" Zoe Ministries, Church Station, Po Box 270, New York, NY 10008 Pg.67-75 1991, 1997

"Confession - Who I Am in God." HopeFaithPrayer. N.p., n.d. Web. 23 Oct. 2014

GIVE A COPY OF THIS BOOK TO YOUR FRIENDS.

THIS IS A PERFECT GIFT TO GIVE TO AN UNSAVED FRIEND OR FAMILY MEMBER.

I Would Like to Hear From You

If you'd like to invite my ministry to minister at your church, at your upcoming Revival service, or to help local ministers fortify their congregations in unity... Or if you have prayed the salvation prayer for the first time, or if you have a testimony to share with me after reading this book, please contact me.

To contact the Author write:

Yves P. Beauvais
Eleventh Hour Ministry, Inc.
PO Box 184
Boca Raton, FL 33429
Toll free: (877)-932-7346
www.ehministry.org
info@ehministry.org
www.pastoryvesonline.org

URGENT PRAYER REQUESTS

Mail your financial seed Gifts and/or three of your <u>most urgent prayer</u> requests and I will agree with you in prayer for change:

1. _____

2. _____

3. _____

I look forward to hearing from you and I want to celebrate with you!

Yves P. Beauvais
Eleventh Hour Ministry, Inc.
PO Box 184
Boca Raton, FL 33429
Toll Free: (877)-932-7346
www.Ehministry.org
<u>www.pastoryvesonline.org</u>